DNA DETECTIVE

WRITTEN BY
TANYA LLOYD KYI

ILLUSTRATED BY
LIL CRUMP

annick press
toronto + new york + vancouver

Cover art by Lil Crump
Cover and interior design by Belle Wuthrich
Edited by Catherine Marjoribanks
Copyedited by Judy Phillips

Annick Press Ltd.

We acknowledge the support of the Canada Council for the Arts, the Ontario Arts Council, and the Government of Canada through the Canada Book Fund (CBF) for our publishing activities.

ONTARIO ARTS COUNCIL
CONSEIL DES ARTS DE L'ONTARIO
an Ontario government agency
un organisme du gouvernement de l'Ontario

Cataloging in Publication

Kyi, Tanya Lloyd, 1973-, author
    DNA detective / Tanya Lloyd Kyi ; illustrated by Lil Crump.

Includes bibliographical references and index.
Issued in print and electronic formats.
ISBN 978-1-55451-773-2 (pbk.).—ISBN 978-1-55451-774-9 (bound)
ISBN 978-1-55451-775-6 (html).—ISBN 978-1-55451-776-3 (pdf)

    1. DNA—Juvenile literature. 2. Genetics—Juvenile literature.
I. Crump, Lil, illustrator II. Title.

QP624.K95 2015   j572.8'6   C2015-900472-1
                                             C2015-900473-X

Published in the U.S.A. by Annick Press (U.S.) Ltd.

Printed in China

Visit us at: www.annickpress.com
Visit Tanya Lloyd Kyi at: www.tanyalloydkyi.com
Visit Lil Crump at: www.ideahousedesign.com

Also available in e-book format. Please visit www.annickpress.com/ebooks.html for more details. Or scan

CONTENTS

INTRODUCTION 3

1 SUPER SLEUTH   7

2 CLUE COLLECTING   24

3 CODE BREAKERS   42

4 HOT ON THE TRAIL   54

5 RED HERRINGS   69

6 WHODUNIT?   88

CONCLUSION 102

FURTHER READING 108

SELECTED SOURCES 109

IMAGE CREDITS 112

INDEX 113

ABOUT THE AUTHOR 116
& ILLUSTRATOR

INTRODUCTION

WHO BROKE INTO the jewelry store? Unfortunately, the thief didn't leave a card at the scene of the crime with a name and contact info. But maybe he or she left something behind that will be just as helpful: DNA evidence.

There are many different kinds of clues that come into play in a criminal investigation: evidence from eyewitnesses, security-camera video, and fingerprints, to name just a few. But sometimes those things are unreliable, or inconclusive, or simply not available. When that's the case, the detective might turn to a tool that's expensive but often more useful: DNA identification.

But what exactly *is* DNA, and how can it solve crimes?

BUILDING BLOCK BASICS

DNA **STANDS FOR A WORD** so long that even scientists don't bother pronouncing it: deoxyribonucleic acid.

In the center of almost every cell in our bodies, there's a piece of DNA, designed to give the body instructions. In human DNA, those instructions say things like: "Create two legs, two arms, two eyes, and one nose." In a lemur's DNA, there are blueprints for a long, striped tail. A rainbow trout's DNA includes a recipe for iridescent scales.

All the instructions to create a person are written in a code about 3 billion units long. And the entire thing has to fit inside the center of a cell.

Which seems impossible! How can so much information be squeezed into such a tiny space?

Well, each DNA molecule is shaped like a spring. Imagine a toy Slinky. If you stretch it out, it might be taller than you are. But when you let it go, it's smaller than your hand. DNA molecules are like microscopic Slinkies. They're twisted so tightly that they can fit inside your cells. But if you took all those spring shapes from your body, joined them, and stretched them, they'd reach to the moon and back . . . six thousand times!

Our DNA molecules are actually double springs, connected by rungs, so that they can carry even more information. They're shaped a lot like spiral staircases. The twisting "handrails" are made of sugar (deoxyribose) and phosphate. The "stairs" are made of four chemical bases called nucleotides: adenine, guanine, cytosine, and thymine. Those chemical names are a mouthful, so everyone calls them by their initials: A, G, C, and T.

Each person's DNA is unique. Yours might make your eyes blue instead of brown. Other pieces might give you extra-fast reflexes, or strange and wiggly ears. It all depends on your own particular code.

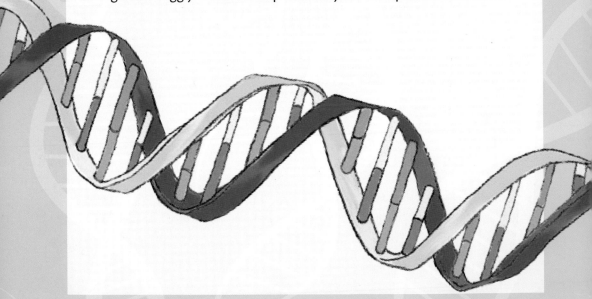

DNA FINGERPRINTS

YOUR DNA and the DNA of your best friend are remarkably similar. In fact, they're 99.9 percent the same. That explains why you both have hair on the top of your head, two eyebrows, two eyes, one nose, and a mouth. But unless you're identical twins, your DNA also has a few pretty obvious differences. You each have 3 billion units of code, after all. So even if only 0.1 percent is different, that's still 3 million units. It's as if each human on earth has a unique barcode.

Parts of the DNA code repeat over and over again, in a pattern. Scientists can look at the patterns and tell which people are related to one another. The repeating patterns of family members, who share a lot of the same DNA, are similar, while those of strangers are usually quite different.

How does this help in a criminal investigation? Well, if crime scene investigators can find even a few cells—in a drop of spit, a single hair, or a smear of blood, for example—they can send the evidence to a lab, where researchers look at the repeating patterns. They enter those patterns into a computer and compare them to the DNA patterns of a suspect. It's like using a high-tech fingerprint to identify a criminal.

Sometimes, evidence hides in unusual places. Detectives have found DNA on the handles of base-ball bats, the licked surfaces of postage stamps, the tips of toothpicks, and the rims of drinking glasses.

SUPER SLEUTH ①

FOR THOUSANDS OF YEARS, humans have understood that traits are passed down through families. Ancient farmers bred their biggest, strongest animals to create big, strong offspring. They knew that by planting the kernels of the tallest, healthiest corn, they were likely to get better crops the following year. And they recognized that two parents with big noses were more likely to have a big-nosed kid.

But they didn't know *why* this was true.

Ancient philosophers took their best guesses:

- SEEDS More than two thousand years ago, a guy named Hippocrates suggested that both men and women produced tiny seeds, which joined to create babies.

- GUTS The Greek philosopher Aristotle said women provided the blood and guts of babies, but men gave them their shape.

- SPIRIT In China, early doctors believed that both mother and father contributed a sort of life energy to create a baby.

There was no way to prove or disprove any of these ideas until the 1600s, when microscopes were invented. Finally, doctors and scientists could see individual cells. They discovered the egg cells of women and the sperm cells of men. And they thought that maybe—just maybe—these cells helped make babies.

So, did they conclude that sperm and egg united, each providing genetic material to the new creature?

No. They spent the next two hundred years arguing. One group of scientists said that the sperm was responsible for a baby's creation, while others insisted that it was the egg.

It seems a bit silly now, but there were good reasons for all this confusion. Sometimes babies looked exactly like their fathers. Sometimes they looked like their mothers. Sometimes people passed crooked ears or funny chins on to their children, and sometimes they didn't. Sometimes a baby was born with disabilities that didn't seem to come from its father or mother. The evidence was a mess!

Fortunately, in the mid-1700s, two men took some important steps toward understanding it all:

- In England, a sheep breeder named Robert Bakewell set out to turn a better profit from barnyard animals. He bred not simply for

strong and healthy animals, but also for those with specific traits that would be valuable in the marketplace. Eventually, he produced sheep with long and shiny wool, meaty bodies, and no sharp horns.

- In France, a mathematician named Pierre Louis Maupertuis traced members of a Berlin family born with extra fingers. Sometimes the trait seemed to be passed from the father, and sometimes from the mother. So Maupertuis suggested that both parents contributed "hereditary particles" to their babies.

Today, the conclusions of these men seem obvious. But that's because we've all grown up with the idea that we inherit Mom's eyes, Dad's nose, and Grandma's temper. In the 1700s, these were significant steps toward understanding genetics.

Spanish royalty from the House of Habsburg had no trouble recognizing a family member in a portrait. Because their intermarrying led to DNA trouble, family members inherited the very prominent "Habsburg jaw". The jaw of King Charles II was so large, his top and bottom teeth didn't meet. He had serious chewing and speaking problems.

BAD BLOOD

BY THE 1800s, people understood that diseases and disorders were sometimes passed on along family lines. The most obvious example in Europe was a condition often called "the royal disease." It was hemophilia, a disorder in which blood doesn't clot properly. People with hemophilia bruise easily and can bleed to death if they're cut or badly bumped. And while females carry the disease, it's usually males who show symptoms.

In Europe, it was several *royal* males.

Queen Victoria had unknowingly passed hemophilia to some of her children, who then passed it to their children. Because the princes and princesses of England married other nobles, the disease spread through the royal families of England, Spain, Germany, and Russia, wreaking havoc along the way. One of Queen Victoria's sons, two grandsons, and six great-grandsons died of the disorder.

People didn't understand exactly how the disease was transmitted, but they knew it passed from parent to child.

ISLAND HOPPING

IDEAS ABOUT HEREDITY began to grow more specific when a young naturalist named Charles Darwin hitched a ride on a boat bound for South America. In 1831, the *Beagle* set sail from England. It would take Charles to the Amazon rainforest, the cliffs of Argentina, and eventually along the equator to the Galápagos Islands, about 970 kilometers (600 miles) west of Ecuador.

Formed by volcanoes rising from the sea, these islands were so far from land that the plants and animals there developed differently from their mainland counterparts. Over thousands of years, they became entirely unique. The islands themselves—eighteen main ones, and several smaller outcroppings—were separated by deep channels that few animals could cross. Charles learned that locals could tell from which island a tortoise came just by looking at the pattern on its shell.

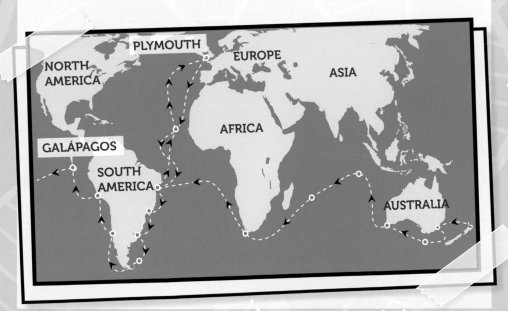

PLYMOUTH

EUROPE

ASIA

NORTH AMERICA

AFRICA

GALÁPAGOS

SOUTH AMERICA

AUSTRALIA

Excited by the variety of unusual creatures, Charles began collecting specimens. He took fish, snails, birds, reptiles, and bugs, labeling them and packing them for transport. By the time he headed back to England in 1836, he had 1,750 pages of notes and more than five thousand biological bits, from feathers to bones. He had everything he needed to—eventually—figure out why and how certain genetic traits were passed along family lines.

BIRDS OF A FEATHER

HOW COULD ONE MAN EXAMINE five thousand samples? There was no way Charles Darwin could get through all that work alone. So he bundled up some of his specimens and sent them off to other experts.

Among his collections were several birds—some with small beaks and some with sharp ones, some found in trees and some found on the

ground. He guessed that these specimens included blackbirds, grosbeaks, and finches. They weren't the most interesting or the most beautiful of his creatures, so Charles sent them to a bird expert to study.

When the expert wrote back to Charles, he said, thanks for all these birds, but they're not really as different as you said they were. They're all various species of finch.

What? All the birds turned out to be members of the same feathered club! How could they look so different if they all had common ancestors? Suddenly, Charles had an idea. Maybe he'd collected each bird from a separate island. Maybe the finches that lived in different environments had specific traits, the same way the tortoises from different islands had unique shells.

Soon, Charles came up with some theories about how animals evolved to suit their environments. But he wasn't yet ready to share his ideas with the world.

Instead, he bought himself a whole lot of pigeons. He joined pigeon clubs and built a pigeon house and wrote to pigeon experts. Why? Well, partly because he fell in love with the amazing variations in the pigeon world. But also because he wanted to prove that the main breeds had all descended from the plain old

DID YA HEAR THAT?
I'M AMAZING!

rock pigeon. He showed that by breeding some birds for color, farmers had produced one species; by breeding them for size, they'd produced another. And so on, and so on.

Charles started with the knowledge that birds inherited traits from their parents and could pass those traits to their offspring. He then connected that idea to his Galápagos research. In the wild, creatures with certain traits were more likely to survive in a specific environment. A finch with a large beak, for example, might be better at cracking nuts. If nuts were the main source of food on an island, then that finch would grow stronger and healthier, have more babies than weaker finches, and pass on its strong beak. Eventually, strong-beaked finches could take over an island.

When he published his book *On the Origin of Species* in 1859, Charles gave this idea a name: *natural selection*. Stronger creatures lived longer and passed on their traits more often.

But he worried that this might not be easily understood, so he borrowed another phrase from a fellow scientist, Herbert Spencer: *survival of the fittest*. The creatures with traits that best "fit" their environments were the strongest. They survived, and passed on their useful traits to the next generation, while others died out.

In all of his research, Charles was exploring genetics. But he still didn't know why traits were sometimes inherited and sometimes not. And where in the body did instructions for a trait live? How, exactly, did a creature pass on a characteristic to its young? For answers to those questions, the world would have to wait.

Today, the Galápagos Islands are part of a national park in Ecuador. To help protect the creatures there, the government allows only a limited number of visitors.

DEVILS AND DETAILS

IN THE MID-1800s, Charles Darwin and other scientists like him were beginning to understand two things. First, that different creatures were uniquely suited to their environments. Second, that diversity—all sorts of animals, each a little bit different—equaled strength. If there were some animals better adapted to cold, then those creatures would survive unusually chilly winters. If some birds were better suited to eating nuts, they could live through seasons with little fruit. And those better-adapted animals would help to keep the whole species from dying out during hard times.

These theories help explain a lot. But they're no help to the Tasmanian devil. About forty thousand years ago, Tasmanian devils lived across Australia. Then the aboriginal people arrived on the continent. With them came wild dogs called dingoes—a new predator. Hunted by dingoes, the devils soon died out. Except on the island of Tasmania.

Tasmania is separated from the mainland of Australia by a wide, deep channel. No one knows exactly how the devils got to the island. And not many made it there. Probably all 150,000 of the animals still living descended from just a few individual ancestors. And because of that, the entire living population is genetically pretty similar.

That genetic similarity is now causing problems. A contagious cancer has attacked the animals, invading their mouths and making it impossible for them to eat.

If the devils were a normal group of animals, each creature would have a wide variety of different, unique genes, some of which might resist the cancer. But the devils share most of the same genes. So, one after another, the animals are dying. Almost two-thirds of them are gone. The species faces extinction.

Not if scientists can help it, though.

Today, wildlife officials are capturing healthy Tasmanian devils and keeping them separate from the wild population to help ensure some of the animals escape the disease. Other scientists are trying to figure out if a few devils might be genetically resistant. If they can find even a small number of animals able to fight off the cancer, they can breed more tumor-resistant devils. It's a small chance, but one that scientists are determined to pursue.

In the meantime, Australian biologists are sending a warning to wildlife officials in other parts of the world: Make sure you have big populations of animals, with lots of genetic diversity. That's the only way wild creatures can be safe from unexpected threats.

CREATURE FEATURES

TAKE A LOOK AROUND YOUR CLASSROOM, or around a local restaurant. There are lots of variations in any handful of people. Even within our families, most of us are a mishmash of features. Maybe your great-aunt says you have your father's nose, or Grandma says you're the spitting image of your mother. Or maybe you have green eyes when both your parents have brown. Our insides are just as variable. Some of us have better immune systems, some of us have larger hearts, and some of us have different wiring in tiny areas of our brains.

So, we know that each of us is an assortment of parts. But how are our traits passed along from one generation to the next? The man who finally figured it out didn't work on something as complicated as people. He studied pea plants. Thousands and thousands of pea plants.

GREGOR THE GARDENER

YOU'RE AN ANXIOUS, INTROVERTED BRAINIAC.
All you want to do is study. But your farming family can't afford to pay for much education. Should you:

- ☑ Work as a gardening beekeeper to support yourself?

- ☑ Spend your sister's dowry on science classes?

- ☑ Join the priesthood?

IF YOU ARE GREGOR MENDEL, THE ANSWER IS: ALL OF THE ABOVE.

After spending every cent on schooling and still not getting his fill, Gregor donned monk's robes in 1843. He then dove into studies of math, physics, and botany.

In 1865, he took the same determination he'd applied to his education and started breeding simple, fast-growing pea plants. He soon figured out that plants inherited traits from their parent plants, and that each trait was passed along separately. For example, a parent plant might have yellow seeds and large leaves. It could pass either or both of these traits along to the next generation. Each trait was like a separate building block that could be used or not used.

Eventually, after studying thousands of plants, Gregor came up with two basic rules:

RULE #1: THE LAW OF SEGREGATION For every trait, we inherit two possibilities, one from the female side and one from the male side. Some of these possibilities are "dominant" and others are "recessive." The dominant possibilities are the ones we are most likely to inherit.

In Mendel's pea plants, there were two possibilities for seed color: yellow or green. Yellow was the dominant color. A plant that inherited yellow from both the male and female sides would certainly produce yellow seeds. A plant that inherited yellow from the male side and green from the female side would still have yellow seeds, because yellow was dominant. It trumped green. But if a plant inherited green from the male side and green from the female side, then the recessive trait would win and the seed color would be green.

RULE #2: THE LAW OF INDEPENDENT ASSORTMENT Different traits can be passed on independently. So, a pea plant could inherit the green leaves of one parent plant without necessarily inheriting its yellow seeds.

Gregor was also sure that inheritance could be predicted with mathematical rules. Today's scientists think he might have made his results a little more regular than they really were, just to fit his perfect math equations. Still, he was on the right track. He set out to share his findings with the world.

First he published his results. There was no response. Then he presented his research to other scientists, and asked others to try the same experiments. No one seemed interested. After years of work, poor Gregor discovered that no one cared about his discoveries. Then he was elected the abbot of his monastery and had no more time for science anyway. He died in 1884 without having found anyone to pursue his ideas about inherited traits. In fact, his research seemed so useless that the other monks burned his notebooks.

Maybe the world just wasn't ready.

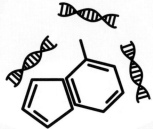

THE LIGHT BULB GOES ON

SIXTEEN YEARS AFTER MENDEL'S DEATH, three other scientists working on separate plant experiments each discovered that plants passed different traits to their offspring independently. When they searched through old science journals, wondering if anyone had looked into this before, they rediscovered Gregor Mendel.

Suddenly, Gregor's old discoveries were big news. And there were more researchers making other discoveries, all pointing the way toward DNA:

- In the 1860s, Swiss doctor Friedrich Miescher studied white blood cells. Inside the center of each cell, the nucleus, he found a chemical goo he called *nuclein*. What he was actually seeing was DNA, though it would be decades before anyone had the powerful tools needed to truly see the molecule's form.

- A Dutch botanist named Hugo de Vries did much of the same research Gregor did, without knowing about Gregor's work. But Hugo didn't conclude that species inherited traits in an orderly, mathematical way. After studying evening primroses, he thought that new species arose through big, sudden mutations. Hugo was wrong with that particular theory, but his work sparked lots of new ideas about inheritance.

- In 1919, a Russian biochemist named Phoebus Levene figured out which chemicals joined together to form DNA.

Slowly, with each new discovery, the world was growing closer to understanding how microscopic codes could hold the instructions for all life.

Where did Friedrich Miescher get his supply of white blood cells?

He scraped the pus from used bandages!

THE SUSPECTS

DEE ZASTER
CASHIER

RUSTY HAMMER
CASHIER

TERRY BILL
CONVICTED THIEF

CAMMIE SOLE
STORE MANAGER

DR.HACKER,DENTIST
REGULAR CUSTOMER

ELLA VADER
LOCAL SECURITY GUARD

STAN STILL
SALES REPRESENTATIVE

DAISY PICKER
OWNS THE STORE NEXT DOOR

DWAYNE PIPE
CUSTODIAN

PIA NUTT
SUPERMODEL,
REGULAR CUSTOMER

HAZEL NUTT
SUPERMODEL,
REGULAR CUSTOMER

IDA GOTTAWAY
STORE BOOKKEEPER

WHERE SHOULD THE INVESTIGATION GO FROM HERE?

HINT: The detective has a DNA "fingerprint" from the glove. What will she need from the suspects?

Answer: A DNA sample

CLUE 2 COLLECTING

IF YOU INHERIT your dad's big ears, you might say, "They're in my genes" or "Big ears are in my DNA." To most of us, those sentences mean pretty much the same thing. Scientifically, though, genes and DNA are at different levels of the same life-building system. There's another level, too, called the chromosome. From smallest to largest, here's what these terms mean:

SMALLEST: DNA DNA molecules are those double springs that look like two handrails (made of sugar and phosphate) connected by nucleotide "stairs" (A, G, C, and T). The DNA molecule provides the code for building the body.

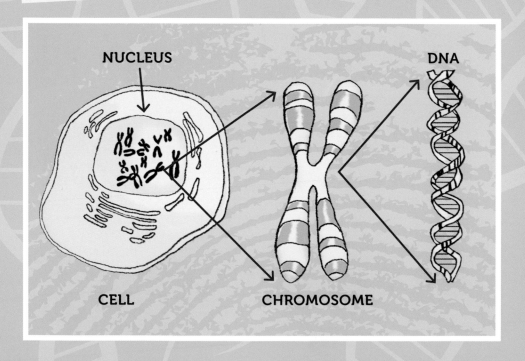

NUCLEUS

DNA

CELL

CHROMOSOME

BIGGER: GENES Genes are snippets or chunks of DNA that carry the building instructions for our different parts. Traits are passed on from parents to children by the work of genes.

BIGGEST: CHROMOSOMES Chromosomes are long strings of DNA molecules wrapped around proteins. Each chromosome contains many genes. Humans have forty-six chromosomes, arranged in pairs.

Where do you find DNA, genes, and chromosomes? If you look at a single cell under a powerful microscope, you'll see a dark spot in the center. That's the nucleus. It's your cell's miniature brain, or command center.

Are you thinking small? Think even smaller! You need a microscope to see a single cell. Then you need an even more powerful microscope to see inside the nucleus. And there probably isn't a microscope at your school that's powerful enough to clearly see a DNA molecule.

MASH-UPS AND MIX-UPS

CELLS MAKE NEW CELLS BY DIVIDING, and every time a cell divides in two, it has to pass its exact DNA code on to the new cell. Now, imagine if someone gave you a code and asked you to handwrite a copy. If it were a page or two long, no problem. But what if the code had 3 *billion* letters, like the units of code in a cell's DNA? You'd probably make a few mistakes along the way.

Cells divide inside you millions of times each day. So it's no surprise that every once in a while something gets copied a little differently from how it should.

MISSING

HAVE YOU SEEN THIS STRAND?

Usually, there are extras of every instruction, which act as insurance against errors. If one tiny chunk of DNA instructs your body to have two eyes, for example, other chunks repeat those instructions. Those repeated codes are in places where your body can double-check itself, to make sure you don't end up with three eyes by accident.

But even with extra checks and double instructions, mistakes still happen. Every once in a while, a major mix-up gets through the system and a mutation occurs. A mutation is a change in the DNA pattern that wasn't supposed to happen.

Mutations can cause all sorts of wild and wonderful things . . .

ALIEN ISLAND

MORE THAN 15 MILLION YEARS AGO, the shoreline of what is now Yemen shifted, and a few pieces of the mainland were pulled farther and farther into the Indian Ocean. They survived as the island of Socotra and three smaller outcroppings nearby.

When it was ripped from the mainland, Socotra took its plants and animals with it. But over millions of years, those plants and animals evolved separately from the ancestors they'd left behind. Eventually, Socotra began to look different from anywhere else on earth. Between the island's desert bowls, mountains, and beaches grew plants that seemed like alien species, and animals that early explorers couldn't identify.

In the 1990s, the United Nations sent a team of researchers to catalog all the plants and animals on the island. They found seven hundred species different from those anywhere else on earth. Those seven hundred species have DNA that changed, over centuries and centuries, until its instructions created entirely unique creatures.

Here are descriptions of just a few of Socotra's otherworldly inhabitants:

- The dragon's blood tree, named for its red sap, has branches that reach up to suck moisture from the island's mountain mists.

- The Chamaeleo monachus has a long, patterned tail and thin, agile limbs. According to local lore, those who hear this lizard's hiss lose their ability to talk.

- Like a shrub from a Dr. Seuss book, the desert rose has a thick trunk to anchor itself to Socotra's rocky cliffs, and hot-pink flowers to attract local pollinating insects.

A rose is a rose, except in Socotra.

Dragon's blood trees evolved over thousands of years. But climate change means temperatures are rising by the decade. Without as much moisture in Socotra's mists, fewer young trees can survive on the rocks. Researchers worry the plant won't adapt quickly enough to survive.

The differences that make these species unique began as random DNA mutations. In some cases, the mutations were just plain mistakes. They weren't particularly helpful, but they weren't damaging either. Other mutations helped the plants and animals survive on their island home. The desert rose, for example, began as an ordinary plant that blooms throughout the region. But on Socotra, the DNA of a few plants said, "Grow bigger." These larger plants were better able to withstand the island's monsoon winds. As more of the big plants survived, passing their DNA to their offspring, the smaller plants died out. And over all those millions of years, the giant desert rose of Socotra kept changing, adapting to its environment, until it became a unique species all its own.

What scientists have seen on Socotra is similar to what Charles Darwin observed in the Galápagos Islands back in the 1830s. There, again over millions of years, plants and animals experienced a lot of random DNA mutations. When the mutations provided an advantage—like a change to the shape of a bird's beak that made it easier to get food—that new trait made it more likely that the plant or animal would survive, and pass that trait on through DNA to the next generation. The plants that were best adapted to the living conditions on the islands and the creatures best able to find food and water and mates eventually took over. This is what Charles called "survival of the fittest."

Places with plentiful food and water support a diversity of plants and animals—even the weaker ones sometimes thrive. But in harsh places, only the creatures most suited to the environment manage to survive.

GENETICS ROCK STAR

GRASSHOPPER GAMES

BY THE EARLY 1900s, scientists had pretty much agreed that traits were inherited. But they were still arguing about *how* those traits were passed from parent to child. There were two main theories:

- Darwin's right! Random changes are happening constantly. The most helpful traits survive while others die out.

- No, *Mendel's* right! Traits are passed along by regular, predictable systems, according to which traits are dominant and which are recessive.

Before they could decide who was right, researchers needed more information about what happens inside cells. The first to contribute some of that knowledge was a farm boy from the wheat fields of Kansas.

Walter Sutton looked as if he belonged tossing
hay bales. He was six feet tall and weighed more than
two hundred pounds. But when his little brother died of
typhoid fever, Walter embarked on a career in medicine
and research.

Some of his early research endeavors still involved the
farm. His first published paper was based on the study of
the grasshoppers he found in his dad's fields. But Walter
went on to study all sorts of creatures, and all sorts of cells.
Collaborating with a researcher named E. B. Wilson, he
began focusing on heredity. Soon he had solved some huge
genetic puzzles. In 1902, he offered major conclusions, including:

- Chromosomes contain genes that provide the code for passing on
  traits.

- Our chromosomes are organized in mother-father pairs. We get half
  our chromosomes from our mothers and half from our fathers.

- The chromosomes we're born with are the ones we keep for our
  whole lives.

Walter learned more than ever before about how traits are passed
along, and he also explained how we humans inherit some of our traits
from our mothers and some from our fathers. The chromosomes in the
centers of our cells are the vehicles for that inheritance.

Y SO DIFFERENT?

HUMANS INHERIT twenty-three pairs of chromosomes from their parents. And most of those pairs are logical and orderly. Only one pair stands out.

Imagine a baby shower, where twenty-two relatives contribute perfectly matching little clothes. A blue shirt and blue pants. A green shirt and green pants. Then one strange relative turns up and gives a purple shirt with orange shorts—something completely different from the other gifts. Something that doesn't match at all!

In the human body, that unmatched set is the twenty-third chromosome pair—and that pair determines whether a baby is a boy or a girl. In a girl, the two chromosomes in the pair are both *X*-shaped. In a boy, there is one *X*-shaped chromosome and one small, mismatched *Y*-shaped chromosome.

But that strange Y has unusual power. One gene on that Y chromosome, called "sex-determining region Y" (SRY), builds a protein

that communicates with the other chromosomes to trigger male
development.

When you were a tiny embryo inside your mother's womb, you were
neither boy nor girl. Not yet. You had tiny reproductive parts that could
become either ovaries (in a girl) or testes (in a boy).

If you're a boy, then something changed at the six-week stage. Your
SRY gene began to produce proteins. And those proteins instructed your
body to become male. If you're a girl, you didn't have a Y chromosome,
so you didn't have an SRY gene. Your body didn't make those special
proteins, and the embryo developed into a female.

That's right—humans become male or female based only on the
activities of one tiny gene and its army of proteins.

FLY GUYS

AT THE BEGINNING of the twentieth century, Thomas Hunt Morgan
worried that science was on the wrong track. He questioned everything.
Whether he was reading arguments for Darwin or arguments for Mendel,
he didn't see hard proof for either theory. And he didn't think Walter
Sutton had gathered enough information for his cell studies. He felt that
no one had methodically shown how inheritance worked.

So, in a small lab at Columbia University, Thomas set out to figure
it out himself. He gathered a group of talented students: Alfred Henry
Sturtevant, Calvin Blackman Bridges, and Hermann Joseph Muller. He
needed to try out his idea on a living creature with a very short life cycle,

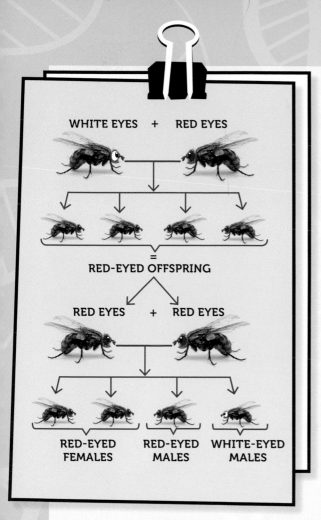

WHITE EYES + RED EYES

↓

= RED-EYED OFFSPRING

RED EYES + RED EYES

↓

RED-EYED FEMALES   RED-EYED MALES   WHITE-EYED MALES

so that he could study as many generations as possible in a short time. So he also gathered fruit flies. *Millions* of them. In the Fly Room, where they worked, his students got cramped desks. The flies got old milk jars and rotting bananas.

In 1910, Thomas and his students found the first random mutation in their flies: a male fly with white eyes.

Thomas's team had found an inherited trait. And they were seeing it *only in males*. The researchers knew that females—whether human or fruit fly—had two *X*-shaped chromosomes, while males had one shaped like an *X* and one shaped like a *Y*. So they guessed (correctly) that if white eyes appeared only in male flies, then the trait must be carried only on the Y chromosome.

Thomas couldn't be skeptical anymore. With more and more fly experiments, he proved to himself, and to the rest of the world, that chromosomes carried the instructions for inheritance. He even proved that certain genes along the strands of chromosomes were responsible for certain traits.

With his fruit flies and banana peels, Thomas had unlocked one of the biggest secrets of genetics. He won a Nobel Prize for his work in 1933.

GENETICS ROCK STAR

BLOODY BRILLIANT

RANDOM GENETIC MUTATIONS helped the plants and animals of Socotra adapt. Other mutations gave white eyes to male fruit flies. All very interesting, but not that useful. Did mutations ever help humans?

In 1949, a guy named J. B. S. (Jack) Haldane suggested that inheriting a disease could sometimes be useful. And that a blood disorder might actually be good for you.

Jack was an all-round genius. He started reading when he was three, worked in his father's biology lab when he was eight, and cowrote his first scientific paper at age twenty. Although he studied math and classics in school, he made major contributions to statistics, biology, physiology, and genetics. He even wrote science fiction stories!

Jack's colleagues (and even friends) thought he was a bit nuts. Why?

- He drank a hydrochloric acid solution to see what it would do to his body.
- He hyperventilated for hours to measure his symptoms.
- In World War I, he snuck behind enemy lines to set bombs.

When it came to the study of blood, Jack came up with a strange theory. He knew that many people in the Mediterranean had fewer red blood cells than normal. No one understood why. But Jack reasoned that having anemia (a lack of red blood cells) might actually protect people

Red blood cells in rush hour

from malaria—always a danger in warm, damp, climates.

Malaria had been a problem for thousands of years, so surely the human body must have had time to evolve and adapt. And some types of anemia were definitely inherited. In those cases, then, could anemia be considered a genetic mutation that gave people a better chance of surviving malaria? Jack also knew that malaria was most dangerous in kids. So, if people without adaptations were killed off young, maybe those with adaptations passed their improved genes to their offspring.

Jack made all these suggestions in the 1940s, before anyone knew with any real accuracy what DNA did. But he was right. Over the following decades, scientists proved that anemia helped combat malaria.

Fewer red blood cells means less oxygen to the body. A type of genetic anemia called sickle cell trait (SCT) can make it dangerous for people to do extreme exercise. After a study in the 1980s showed that recruits with SCT were thirty-seven times more likely to collapse in training, the US Army drew up new rules about hydration and rest breaks.

And even though anemia itself can cause health problems, the trade-off was genetically worthwhile in areas of the world where malaria was common.

Today, doctors can treat anemia, boosting a person's red blood cell count and energy levels. But thanks to Jack's theories and later research, those doctors also know that, sometimes, it's best to let the disorder go untreated.

A COLORFUL CHARACTER

IN 1990, a man named Emerson Moser retired from Crayola Crayons. He'd worked for the company for thirty-seven years, from the time when each crayon was made by hand to the time when seventy-two colors were mixed and molded by machine. He'd seen a lot of changes—but not always the same way other workers had seen them. Emerson Moser, chief crayon maker, was color-blind. Sometimes he had to check with his fellow workers to find out if he was pouring the right hue in the right place.

Like anemia, color blindness can be an inherited genetic condition. In 1986, scientists found the exact genes that control our ability—or

inability—to see the usual spectrum of colors. In Emerson Moser (or his ancestors), the DNA that makes up those genes was somehow copied a little bit differently.

Emerson lived a long and happy life despite his DNA mutation. That change in his gene occurred in a spot where the results weren't *too* serious. But what if copying errors happen in crucial places?

BEFORE HIS TIME

IN 1996, Sam Berns was born a kicking, crying, seemingly normal baby boy. But a year later, his parents were back in the doctor's office, worried about their son. He wasn't thriving. His skin seemed unusually tight, stretching over his joints.

When Sam was only twenty-two months old, doctors diagnosed a rare genetic condition called progeria—the "aging disease." It's incredibly rare. When Sam was diagnosed, there were only about a hundred known sufferers around the world. These kids aged at an accelerated rate. As toddlers, they lost their hair, and their joints became less stable. As children, they developed heart disease as if they were eighty-year-olds. There were no medicines available. There was no cure. Most

Sam with his Boston Bruins hero Zdeno Chara at Progeria Awareness Night

sufferers died when they were about thirteen years old, usually from heart attack or stroke.

Doctors broke the news: Sam would age and die at super-speed.

But Sam's parents, Scott Berns and Leslie Gordon, weren't ready to return home quietly and face that news. Scott was a pediatrician and Leslie was studying to become one. Within a couple of years, they'd created the Progeria Research Foundation, and set out to find treatments for their son and other kids like him.

In 2003, a team that included Sam's mother compared the genes of progeria sufferers with the genes of their parents. They found a mutation in a gene called LMNA, which produces proteins needed by cells. In 2009, doctors started testing the first possible medicines for the condition, using a drug that was originally developed for cancer treatment.

Sam, meanwhile, pursued his dreams. He was an avid drummer. In high school, he desperately wanted to play in the marching band. But the snare drum and harness weighed almost as much as Sam himself. He and his family hired an engineer to redesign the drum and created one that weighed only three kilograms (six pounds). Soon, Sam was marching with his bandmates.

When Sam told this and other stories at a TED conference, the video went viral. Sam Berns died on January 10, 2014, at the age of seventeen, but his video still inspires people around the world. The charity founded by his family continues to fund genetic research in hopes of giving other progeria sufferers longer, healthier lives.

DNA IN THE DEPTHS

THE WORK OF WALTER SUTTON and Thomas Hunt Morgan had proven that Gregor Mendel was right—parents passed their traits to their offspring in a generally predictable pattern. But Darwin was also right. When a random mutation helped a creature survive, that creature would pass its genes to its offspring and, eventually, those adapted offspring could take over. Finches with super-strong beaks could rule an island of the Galápagos. Trees with moisture-sucking branches could spread across the island of Socotra.

Sometimes, scientists find even more bizarre examples of creatures that have adapted to unique environments. For example:

- BROWN KIWIS To help them sniff out underground insects, these New Zealand birds have developed nostrils at the end of their beaks.

A kiwi (the bird, not the fruit)

- SUNDA PANGOLINS These anteater-like creatures from Southeast Asia dine on termites. To better slurp the insects from their mounds, they have evolved to have a super-long tongue that stretches all the way from a bone near the pelvis.

- ICEFISH These Arctic-dwelling fish absorb oxygen straight from the ocean. They don't need red blood cells to fuel their muscles.

Millions of years ago, icefish functioned like we do. Scientists know this because the fish still have a gene that—if it worked—would help build blood cells. But since the fish found a useful mutation, one that gave them a plentiful supply of direct oxygen, the blood-cell gene fell out of use. Now that unused gene is simply a remnant of the species' genetic past.

WHICH SUSPECT WILL THE DETECTIVE ELIMINATE?

HINT: Remember, this case isn't black and white—and neither were the contents of the jewelry cases.

CODE BREAKERS ③

YOU CAN TAKE THE RESULTS of your own genetic testing to a "portrait" company to create artwork from your personal pattern. You'll receive a glowing barcode of colored stripes to hang on your wall. You can even choose the color palette, the size, and the frame.

Obviously, our ability to visualize DNA has come a long way. Just a hundred years ago, scientists had no idea what it looked like. They knew it lived in the center of cells. They knew it controlled heredity. But they didn't know its size, shape, or form. DNA was simply too small to see under the microscopes available at that time.

Then came the field of X-ray crystallography. We usually think of X-rays as tools for diagnosing broken bones. But X-rays are actually a lot like light. Just as you can bounce light off a mirror, researchers learned to bounce and scatter X-rays off crystals. Then they used the pattern made by the bouncing rays to trace the shape of the crystal. When scientists want to study the shape of a particular molecule, they take a sample of the molecules in a solution, mix it with a special liquid to form tiny droplets, and then let the liquid evaporate. At that point, the solution becomes more concentrated and a three-dimensional crystal pattern forms. Not all molecules easily take crystal form but, luckily for the researchers, DNA molecules do!

Figuring out the form of a molecule through X-ray crystallography is like looking at a bunch of overlapping reflections—a bit tricky, in other words. It would take several expert X-ray bouncers to decode the images of DNA crystals and create pictures of the genetic code for the very first time. Then it would take several more scientists to turn those images into a model that everyone could see and understand.

GENETICS ROCK STAR

X-RAY EXPERT

AS A LITTLE GIRL IN THE 1930s, Rosalind Franklin attended St. Paul's Girls' School in London, England, one of the only schools in the city that taught science to girls. Rosalind learned the basics of biology and chemistry while still in elementary school.

And that was lucky, because Rosalind's love of science grew and grew. She'd grow up to become one of the most important researchers in the field of genetics.

After she earned her PhD at Cambridge University, she moved to Paris. There she became an expert in X-ray crystallography. Mostly, she made pictures of viruses. She gained renown in her field, publishing almost fifty papers and speaking at events around the world. When she started making pictures of DNA too, she shared those images with another researcher, named Maurice Wilkins.

Rosalind wasn't the first person to create an image of DNA through X-ray crystallography. But earlier images were so blurry and confusing, scientists couldn't quite figure out what they were looking at. Many tried to make models of shapes that would explain all those reflections and shadows, but none of the models made sense.

Rosalind's pictures were different. She showed that there were two different forms of DNA crystals, which she called the A form and the B form. In early images, those forms were mixed, but Rosalind had managed to capture one form at a time. In her images, DNA appeared more clearly than ever before. She could see that:

- Each strand had two "backbones" with chemicals attached.
- One backbone and its chemicals held a pattern that started at the top and went down.
- The other backbone's pattern started at the bottom and went up.

She'd discovered that the two DNA backbones were like mirror images of each other—a discovery that changed the way scientists thought about the code, and about the structure of the molecule itself.

Then, tragically, Rosalind died of cancer. She was only thirty-seven years old. Her tombstone reads: "Her work on viruses was of lasting benefit to mankind." Which was true. But in 1958, no one yet recognized what an amazing thing Rosalind had begun by creating images of DNA. In fact, most people still didn't know that DNA existed. So no one predicted that while Rosalind's work on viruses would be mostly forgotten, her work on DNA would become famous around the world.

SPLITTING STRANDS

ROSALIND CAPTURED HER IMAGES of DNA as it was stretched thin, the way it might be just before it was replicated inside a cell. Every second, your body makes millions of new cells. It does this by dividing its existing cells. Inside each cell, the information is carefully copied. Then—*pop!* The cell splits itself into two.

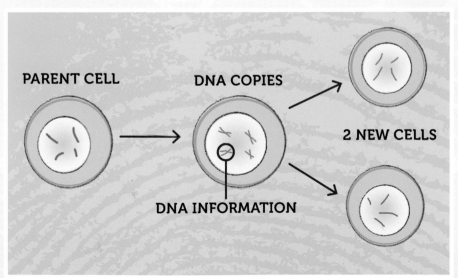

PARENT CELL

DNA COPIES

2 NEW CELLS

DNA INFORMATION

A proofreader has checked every word of this book. In the same way, the enzymes in your cells check and double-check their DNA copying. Scientists call this "exonucleolytic proofreading."

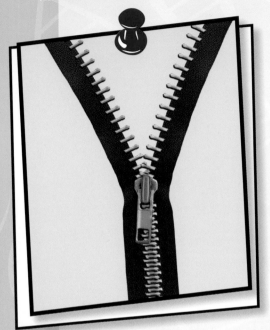

But copying DNA is a tricky thing. Before a cell divides, 3 billion units of code must be reproduced.

Fortunately, there are microscopic "factory workers" called enzymes to do the grunt work inside each cell. First, they detach the two DNA backbones, separating them the way you might separate the two sides of a zipper. Then they begin to meticulously copy.

Attached to each strand of DNA are the four bases: A, T, C, and G (adenine, thymine, cytosine, guanine). An A always connects to a T, and a C always connects to a G. The enzymes set to work creating the correct base to match each unit of code. When they reach an A, they build a T. When they see a C, they build a G. And when they're finished, they've created a mirror image of each backbone. There are now two strands of DNA. Each strand has one "mother" side and a new "daughter" side. Once the DNA is copied, the cell can divide. One cell has become two, each with its matching DNA.

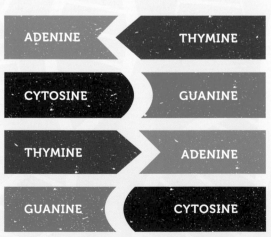

ADENINE	THYMINE
CYTOSINE	GUANINE
THYMINE	ADENINE
GUANINE	CYTOSINE

GENETICS ROCK STAR

SHUTTERBUGS

WHILE ROSALIND SPENT her childhood studying science, Maurice Wilkins spent his youth building instruments. He loved microscopes and telescopes, and even made his own lenses. As an adult, Maurice put these skills to use as the head of a biophysics unit at King's College in London, England. He designed his own equipment for separating tiny DNA fibers, and his own cameras for photographing them. Like Rosalind, he was an expert in X-ray crystallography. And like Rosalind, he captured increasingly clear images.

He was convinced that DNA was shaped like a spiral. If he took enough X-rays, he was sure he could prove it.

In 1950, Maurice took his best images to a conference, where he showed them to an enthusiastic young scientist named James Watson. When Rosalind sent Maurice a particularly great DNA image that she'd captured, Maurice passed that one along too.

He was sharing the best collection of DNA images ever produced.

A MAN, A PLAN, A CANAL —PANAMA!

PALINDROMES read the same forward or backward. They can be single words, such as *mom* and *dad*. Or they can be longer phrases, such as *never odd or even*.

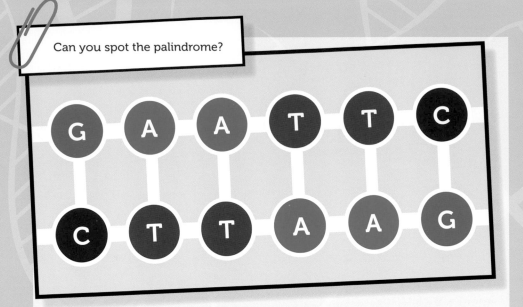

Can you spot the palindrome?

Palindromes don't exist only in English. They've been found in ancient Roman, Hebrew, and Sanskrit texts. They're popular in poetry in many parts of the world, and in pop culture. There are even Pokémon characters with palindrome names.

As researchers learned more about DNA, they could see that the long strands—the railings of the spiral staircase—were joined by the chemical bases called A, G, C, and T. And as they looked more closely, they could see that those bases were arranged in patterns. For example, one section might read G-A-A-T-T-C, while a mirrored piece might read C-T-T-A-A-G.

Scientists realized they were seeing a code within the human body, and much of that code was written in palindromes.

Some people see art as well as science in the palindrome patterns of DNA. Religious leaders often point to the perfect microscopic spirals and repeating poem-like codes within our cells as evidence a supreme being created life on earth.

GENETICS ROCK STAR

A PERSISTENT PAIRING

AMERICAN RESEARCHER JAMES WATSON had two degrees in biology by the time he was twenty-three years old. He took a job at Cambridge University in London in 1951, then traveled to a conference in Italy, where he saw Maurice Wilkins's images of DNA.

He was fascinated.

He rushed back to Cambridge and convinced a man named Francis Crick to help him create a model showing exactly what DNA looked like. Francis was supposed to be studying X-ray crystallography and blood cells, but James was persuasive. Soon, the two were immersed in the latest DNA research. They gathered bits of information from scientists all over the world. It was like trying to build a thousand-piece puzzle when different scientists had different puzzle pieces—and a few pieces were missing altogether. Many people—including Maurice Wilkins—told them they were crazy to try.

But James and Francis were determined. They collected all the pieces they could:

- Thanks to Rosalind Franklin and Maurice Wilkins, they had images of DNA crystals.

- After meeting an Austrian-American biochemist

named Erwin Chargaff, they learned one of "Chargaff's rules": There were equal numbers of A and T bases in DNA, and equal numbers of G and C.

- American chemist and activist Linus Pauling (who later won a Nobel Prize in Chemistry *and* a Nobel Peace Prize) had shown that some protein molecules in blood cells were shaped like helixes, or spirals.

Taking all this information and more, James and Francis set out to create a model of what DNA looked like. They came up with an initial version and eagerly invited their fellow scientists to view it. Rosalind saw it and scoffed. It would never stick together if it were formed like that, she said. In fact, reactions to their draft model were so terrible that the college asked James and Francis to please stop building examples until more information was found.

But they didn't. They kept researching and thinking and building until they arrived at what they were *sure* was the true shape of DNA. Their final model was a double helix (a spiral-staircase shape). They showed the way the two long strands could stretch and split to be copied, then rejoin into a spiral once again. And they showed that the ladder rungs inside the staircase were units of code.

Francis felt that he and James were on the brink of something amazing.

Francis went home one day and told his wife he'd made a huge, world-changing discovery. She just nodded and smiled. Apparently, he said things like that all the time.

SHAPE SHIFTING

IMAGINE BUILDING the most complicated house of cards the world has ever seen, then asking your best friend to make an exact copy of it. Except instead of giving your friend your house to look at, you give him photographs of its shadows.

That's sort of what James and Francis had to do—make a model of one of the most complicated shapes in the universe, using pictures of the shape's scattered X-rays. They built their model with an array of brass rods and balls and a collection of ring stands from their labs—thin metal stands with clamps attached. When it was finished, the whole thing looked like a giant construction of Tinkertoys.

Time magazine sent a young photographer named Antony Barrington Brown to take a picture of the two scientists with their finished model. Antony had no idea what DNA was, and no idea what their discovery meant. But he told the men to stand in front of their model and look important. He snapped the shot.

Although Antony was paid for his photo, it wasn't used for a long time. Then, all of sudden, the world realized what a massive discovery James and Francis had really made. They'd created an image of the building blocks of human life. They were famous. And so was Antony's photo.

James (left) and Francis (right) showing off their model marvel

GAIN AND GLORY

WHILE JAMES AND FRANCIS were busy building models, Rosalind Franklin also had figured out the true shape of DNA. She wrote two papers explaining the spiral-staircase idea. At least one of these was written before she saw the model made by James and Francis, and the three of them were all published in the same scientific journal at the same time.

So, who discovered the true shape of DNA? Well, James and Francis would never have figured it out without the images produced by Rosalind and Maurice. But other people wouldn't have understood it nearly as well without the model made by James and Francis.

In 1962, James, Francis, and Maurice earned a Nobel Prize for discovering the structure of DNA. Unfortunately, Rosalind Franklin had no share in the glory—she'd died four years before, and only living people can receive the Nobel Prize.

WHICH SUSPECT DID NOT HAVE TO BE ASKED FOR A DNA SAMPLE?

DEE ZASTER
CASHIER

RUSTY HAMMER
CASHIER

TERRY BILL
CONVICTED THIEF

CAMMIE SOLE
STORE MANAGER

ELLA VADER
LOCAL SECURITY GUARD

STAN STILL
SALES REPRESENTATIVE

DAISY PICKER
OWNS THE STORE NEXT DOOR

DWAYNE PIPE
CUSTODIAN

PIA NUTT
SUPERMODEL,
REGULAR CUSTOMER

HAZEL NUTT
SUPERMODEL,
REGULAR CUSTOMER

IDA GOTTAWAY
STORE BOOKKEEPER

HINT: In most parts of the world, police can ask for (and keep on file) DNA evidence from people arrested for or convicted of serious crimes.

Answer: Terry Bill

HOT ON THE TRAIL

4

AHOY, MATEY! What's say you and me make ourselves a treasure map? We be lookin' for a gene to cure all the ills of humanity, and X marks the spot!

Well, maybe the geneticists didn't talk like pirates. But they *did* set out to make a treasure map. In the 1980s, a team of scientists decided to map all the genes in human DNA. Together, the genes in the human body are known as the "genome," so the researchers called their quest the Human Genome Project.

Not all the bits of code in our DNA form genes. Much of that code is instructions for turning genes on and off, or it's extra, unused material. The genes themselves are pieces of DNA associated with inherited traits. Remember the ladder shape of DNA, with rungs between the strands? Our genes are groups of ladder rungs.

As they embarked on the Human Genome Project, scientists hoped to catalog our genes and create a sort of treasure map for doctors and

researchers all over the world. Need to identify the genes responsible for sight? Here's where to look. Want to test treatments for diabetes? Here's the gene associated with diabetes. The project would reveal so much genetic information, and share it with so many labs around the world, that many speculated it would soon end disease, starvation, and suffering.

At least, that's what they imagined.

But there were problems deciding who would do the research, who would get the credit, and who would be allowed to make money from the results. And then there were the results themselves.

The human genome itself turned out to be much more complicated than anyone had expected.

FLY TRACKS

BACK IN THE FLY ROOM in 1911, one of Thomas Hunt Morgan's students, Alfred Sturtevant, tracked a mutated gene as it was passed from generation to generation of fruit flies. To make it easier to find and track

This is a simplified version of Alfred's gene map. The chromosome is represented by the long white bar. The vertical colored bars show the locations of the mutated genes.

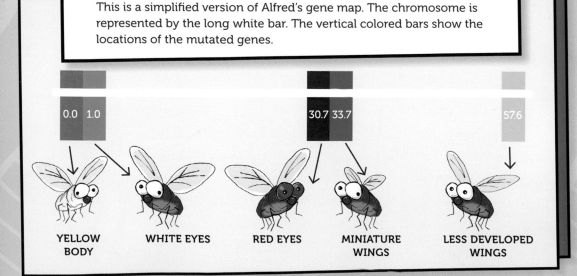

| 0.0 1.0 | | 30.7 33.7 | | 57.6 |

| YELLOW BODY | WHITE EYES | RED EYES | MINIATURE WINGS | LESS DEVELOPED WINGS |

the mutation, Alfred created a diagram. It showed how the gene was constructed (which of the four chemical bases appeared, in what order) and where it occurred along the DNA strand.

This was the very first DNA map.

But Alfred tracked only one gene. To track more, and figure out the order in which they appeared, would take a mastermind of patterns.

GENETICS ROCK STAR

PROTEIN POWER

ONE NOBEL PRIZE wasn't enough for Frederick Sanger: this overachiever won two.

He earned his first for his discoveries about insulin, the hormone that helps our bodies regulate sugar and fat. Until Frederick's research, scientists thought the proteins in insulin were just little clouds of material that floated around, in no particular order. Frederick proved otherwise. He found a distinct pattern within the proteins, like a fingerprint.

That may seem like a tiny detail, but it was an important one. The idea that proteins formed patterns won Frederick the Nobel Prize in Chemistry in 1958. In turn, this research helped Francis Crick (the guy working on DNA models) to discover that the ladder rungs in DNA were also distributed in meaningful patterns—codes that instructed the body to make certain shapes of proteins. Without Frederick's work, James Watson and Francis Crick couldn't have built their DNA model.

But Frederick wasn't finished. In the 1970s, he worked with another scientist, Alan Coulson, to take X-ray pictures of DNA and record the patterns along an individual strand. They examined the "ladder rungs" in the DNA of a bacterium and recorded its sequence of 5,386 bases. In 1977, Frederick found an even faster way of recording the patterns—that was the discovery that earned him his second Nobel Prize in Chemistry.

SEQUENCING SCRAMBLE

IF ALFRED COULD TRACE a fruit fly gene, and Frederick could track DNA patterns, then the world's best scientists should be able to map the entire human genome, right? That was the theory behind the Human Genome Project.

The U.S. government provided funding to an organization called the National Center for Human Genome Research so it could start the

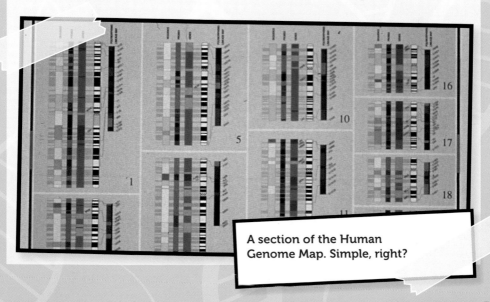

A section of the Human Genome Map. Simple, right?

The Human Genome Project was designed to provide information to *all* doctors and researchers. Scientists released each day's discoveries to the world, free of charge.

work. The project also drew top genetics researchers from around the world. Since no one team could do the huge job alone, labs from Britain, Japan, France, Germany, and China signed on to contribute. Some worked on new research methods to make the mapping process faster. Others worked on individual genes.

But in 1998, a group called the Celera Corporation realized that if it could use faster sequencing techniques, it might be able to decode the human genome first, before the government-funded labs of the world. And that might give the corporation some major advantages.

A private company would have the option to hold on to whatever information it gathered while considering how to profit from it—unlike the government-funded labs, which released their information to the public every day. Other scientists would still get access to the information fairly quickly. But if a company could catalog all the human genes, maybe it could charge scientists to search the catalog. Or, if it was first to identify certain disease-inducing genes, maybe it could develop, produce, and sell the drugs to treat genetic diseases.

Some people liked the idea. Corporate research was almost always faster than government research. Maybe getting drug companies involved would mean quicker, better treatments for genetic diseases.

But as news of Celera Corporation's plans spread, other people began to worry. If private companies were allowed to claim specific research rights, or withhold genetic information from the public, would that lead to corporations *owning* human genes?

ETHICAL DILEMMAS

IF A CORPORATION INVESTS the time and money to invent a machine or create a medicine, that corporation owns the result. It gets a patent, a sort of international claim certificate, which means no one else can steal its ideas. The corporation then has the exclusive right to sell its machine or drug and make a profit.

So, if a corporation invests a lot of time and money to investigate a gene, instead of a machine, shouldn't it still get a patent? Shouldn't it be the only one allowed to develop medicines or treatments based on that gene, so it can make its money back?

If thousands of corporations helped to figure out what genes do, that would benefit people everywhere. But without patents, and the chance to make money on treatments, there would be no motivation for corporations to decode genes. Discovery should equal ownership.

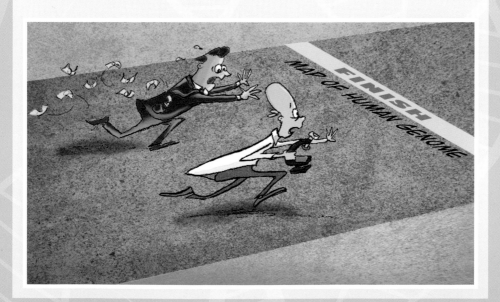

Those were the arguments of people who believed private companies would do the best job of gene research.

The scientists of the Human Genome Project thought differently. They believed that gene research should be available free to everyone—free to researchers working in tiny, underfunded labs, and free to major corporations doing drug research.

These scientists grew so concerned that a private company might claim ownership of genes that they sped up the entire Human Genome Project. Then they sped it up again. They spurred developments in computer technology so the mapping would go faster. And with each increase in efficiency, they posted more and more information online. All for free. In 2000, researchers revealed a draft map of the entire genome.

By 2001, the international research group and Celera were basically tied. There would be no clear winner in the Human Genome Race. They called a truce and jointly released a working draft (like a rough copy) of their research. And in 2003, the international researchers declared their map of the genome complete. Thanks to their speedy work, scientists around the world could freely download the human genome. Celera, meanwhile, began researching personalized medicine—tests and treatments designed specifically to suit a patient's unique genetic code.

Companies continued to claim individual genes for research. But in June 2013, the U.S. Supreme Court declared that DNA in its natural form can't be patented. Other courts around the world are still debating the issue, but most seem to be following the U.S. lead.

So you're in luck: the genes within your body belong entirely to you. Private companies can research human genes and create medicines to affect them, but they can't *own* parts of your DNA.

Opponents of gene patents say that DNA is the basis of life, and life is not a product to be bought or sold.

THE BOOK OF GENOME

BY THE TIME the Human Genome Project was declared complete, scientists had identified about 24,000 genes. This was far fewer than they'd originally imagined. It turned out that mice and flies have almost as many genes as humans. And research on chimpanzees showed that these primates have DNA that is almost identical to ours.

Our close relationship to other creatures was only one of the secrets revealed by the genome. Francis Collins was the director of the National Human Genome Research Institute (the renamed National Center for Human Genome Research) in the United States. He said the genome could be seen as three different types of book:

- a history book about the development of the species;
- a shop manual, with instructions for creating humans;
- a medical textbook, offering new methods of disease prevention and treatment.

Even before the complete map was revealed, researchers were already poring over the details of individual genes, hoping to find the secrets of human development.

GENE DREAMS

CHAMPION GENE

WHICH GENE MAKES PEOPLE ATHLETIC? If researchers could pinpoint that one, maybe they could figure out which kids would grow up to be Olympic athletes. Eventually, they could even tweak that gene in non-athletic people, and make the entire human race more fit.

Or maybe not.

Despite numerous studies, no single gene for athleticism could be found. Scientists failed to isolate a gene for hand-eye coordination, or a gene for stamina, or a gene for strength. In 2011, a project called HERITAGE put almost one hundred families through the following process:

- gene check;
- lots of exercise for five months;
- gene check.

They found that some families got a little more fit during their months of exercise, while other families got a lot more fit. The amount that people's aerobic ability improved seemed to depend on their genes. But not on one gene. Instead, researchers found twenty-one genes tied to improvements in fitness.

The findings in the HERITAGE project were echoed by other scientists in other fields. There didn't seem to be one gene for height and one for bushy eyebrows, one for creativity and one for math skills. Instead, genes interacted and overlapped. Some genes had instructions for many different functions.

The Human Genome Project may have created a map, but that map didn't necessarily lead to a single destination.

?

GREAT GRANDPA GENGHIS

HUMAN DNA is more than 99 percent the same for all of us. If scientists took a sample from you and a sample from Adam Levine, or J. K. Rowling, or the Dalai Lama, they'd look almost the same. But since we have 3 billion units of code, even a half a percent of difference leads to plenty of variation.

Once the Human Genome Project was complete, researchers started comparing people's genes. They started linking ancestry and tracing human migration (and mutation) back through time. Here are some of the surprising things they discovered:

- People with ancestors from central and southern Africa have more variations in their DNA than do people from anywhere else in the world. Geneticists believe this is because humans have lived in Africa for far longer than they've lived elsewhere, and more time equals more cross-breeding and more opportunity for variation.

- Outside of Africa, every single population on earth seems to have descended from the same ancestors—probably a few hundred adventurers who left Africa less than a million years ago.

- Once people settled in different parts of the globe, divided by mountains and rivers, their DNA began to evolve separately. Eventually, the DNA of people in Scandinavia had entirely different mutations than did the DNA of those in South America.

Sometimes, geneticists can even track people's genes back to a single forebear. They've traced the genes of 16 million Asian men back to one male ancestor, for example. And historians think great-grandpa is probably Genghis Khan, who conquered most of Asia in the 1100s and 1200s.

Genghis Khan had hundreds of wives and countless children—plenty of chances to spread his genes around.

THE DATING POOL

IF TWO PEOPLE with different gene mutations have a baby, that baby will likely not inherit either of those mutations. The child will inherit genes from its mother to balance the gene mutations of its father, and vice versa. It's part of the body's double-checking process. We have extra copies of our DNA instructions to help make sure we're born healthy.

Unless . . . our parents have identical mutations.

Closely related parents might both carry recessive genes for the same ailments and deformities, and increase the likelihood of passing them on. This can happen in isolated places where populations are small and families intermarry often. Places like the fishing outposts of Newfoundland. There, a high number of people suffer from a rare heart condition. Doctors diagnosed a problem with the pumping of the right ventricle, but they didn't know how to cure it, or how to diagnose it in advance. Sometimes, there were no symptoms until a patient dropped dead. And that happened fairly often—50 percent of men with the disease and 5 percent of women died before they reached the age of forty.

Eventually, doctors figured out how to implant a tiny machine beside the heart. If someone's heartbeats grew too irregular, or stopped, the machine would shock the heart back into action. But for the machine to be useful, doctors needed to know which Newfoundland residents were at risk.

That's where genetic researchers came in.

In 2007, thanks to the Human Genome Project, they found the gene mutation responsible for the problem. Then they set out to find families who carried the gene. Today, members of those families can have their genes tested long before they experience any heart symptoms. That way, doctors can implant the heart-shocking machine for the people who need it.

For Newfoundland residents, the Human Genome Project and the medical research that came after it meant that fewer people died young, and more families lived long lives together.

THE ICELAND APP

IT'S A CRISP, MOONLIT NIGHT. When Ari and Anna lock eyes at a party, it's love at first sight. They share a romantic kiss on the streets of Reykjavík.

The next day, Ari heads off to his family reunion, eager to tell his parents about the new love of his life. But wait . . . what's Anna doing at his party?

She's his second cousin?!?

Gross!

Does this scene sound unlikely? Well, things like this happen more than you'd think in Iceland. The island nation has only 326,000 people, most from families who've lived there for countless generations. That means many people in Iceland have tons of cousins. So many cousins, they can't keep track of them all.

People don't want to accidentally date their relatives. And genetically, it's a bad idea. Cousins are more likely to have genes with the same mutations, and their kids can inherit genetic problems.

Smartphones to the rescue.

Three University of Iceland engineering students designed an app. Now when two people bump their phones together, the app analyzes their family trees and tells them whether or not they're cousins—*before* they start dating.

There are plenty of fish in the Icelandic sea. And now everyone knows which fish are safe to date.

MORE PRELIMINARY RESULTS FROM THE LAB. FIRST OF ALL, THE SUSPECT HAS TWO X CHROMOSOMES.

GREAT. THAT TAKES FOUR MALES OFF THE LIST.

THERE'S MORE. THE TESTS SHOW GENETIC HERITAGE. THE SUSPECT HAS 100 PERCENT SCANDINAVIAN ANCESTRY.

HMM ... PEOPLE IN SCANDINAVIA EVOLVED SEPARATELY FROM THOSE IN THE REST OF EUROPE. ISOLATED BY OCEAN AND MOUNTAINS. I KNOW WHAT THAT MEANS.

WHO CAN YOU REMOVE FROM THE SUSPECT LIST?

DEE ZASTER
CASHIER

RUSTY HAMMER
CASHIER

IDA GOTTAWAY
STORE BOOKKEEPER

CAMMIE SOLE
STORE MANAGER

ELLA VADER
LOCAL SECURITY GUARD

STAN STILL
SALES REPRESENTATIVE

DAISY PICKER
OWNS THE STORE NEXT DOOR

DWAYNE PIPE
CUSTODIAN

PIA NUTT
SUPERMODEL, REGULAR CUSTOMER

HAZEL NUTT
SUPERMODEL, REGULAR CUSTOMER

HINT: If the criminal has two X chromosomes and Scandinavian ancestry, *she* probably has classic northern European coloring: fair skin and blonde hair.

Answer: Dee Zaster, Rusty Hammer, Ida Gottaway, Stan Still, Daisy Picker, and Dwayne Pipe

RED HERRINGS

WHEN GREGOR MENDEL CROSSED pea plant varieties in the 1800s, he was experimenting with DNA. He was taking genes from one variety of pea plant and giving them to another. He just didn't know it. He could see the end results, but not the genes involved.

Modern geneticists have a lot more science at their fingertips. They can identify individual genes and transfer them between plants to create new, specially designed products. This has led to an array of genetically modified organisms, from the corn in your breakfast cereal to the soybeans in your stir-fry sauce. (There are even genetically modified pets on the market!)

Researchers are also learning more about DNA copies and clones. They're exploring the genetic similarities and differences between twins to see which of our human characteristics are caused by genes, and which by our environments. They're even making their own multiples. Labs can now clone mice, pigs, and sheep so scientists can do research on animals with identical DNA.

WHO'S YOUR STYLIST?

Scientists have removed a hair-growth gene from the mouse on the left.

Soon, scientists may be able to do things that once seemed impossible: cure spinal cord injuries, save endangered species, and bring extinct creatures back to life. Only one thing's for sure: in his pea-plant garden of 1865, Gregor could never have dreamed of the possibilities humans are exploring today.

EARTHY EXPERIMENTS

MONSANTO, AN AMERICAN-OWNED multinational chemical company, was the first to genetically modify a plant cell, in 1982. The company was exploring a field called "biotechnology": combining biology and technology to revolutionize farming. By 1996, Monsanto had released three new products:

- cotton seeds with built-in protection against insects;
- soybeans that thrived while herbicides killed surrounding weeds;
- a hormone to make dairy cows produce more milk.

Other companies quickly followed Monsanto's lead. Together, they made plenty of arguments in favor of genetically modified organisms (GMOs):

- GMOs produce more food, faster. They can feed the hungry around the world.
- GMOs resist pests, so farmers can use less poison.
- GMOs can be engineered to need less water, so droughts won't cause crop failures.

The perfect milk machine?

For some people, genetically modified plants might prove to be life-changing. Imagine you've suffered for years from diabetes. Then one day you see your doctor and get this prescription: Lettuce.

It just might happen.

Professor Henry Daniell in Florida has spent years developing a kind of lettuce that provides insulin. Instead of relying on daily injections, people with diabetes might one day munch a few lettuce leaves and receive enough insulin to keep their bodies running smoothly. The leaves could even be dried and packaged.

Not only is this easier than traditional treatments, it's much cheaper. In some developing countries, the cost of diabetes medicine is half of what the average person earns. So far, studies on insulin lettuce have been done on mice, not people. But if the treatment for diabetes becomes lettuce leaves instead of costly medicine, thousands of lives could be saved.

NOT SO FAST

GMO-FREE!

Non-GMO Verified!

Have you ever seen those lines on food packages? If GMOs are fast-growing, insect-repelling, and safe, why doesn't everyone want to eat them?

Well, there are plenty of people who think scientists have gone overboard with their plant genetics. Organic farmers and health activists say people should be eating pure, natural food, not genetically modified crops. They say no one knows for sure whether GMOs are safe.

Why not? For one thing, genes are usually responsible for more than one function in an organism. Some people fear that when scientists take

It's "Just Say No to GMO" at this protest march.

genes from one plant and stick them in another, they may get more than they expect. What if a toxin is accidentally introduced, causing cancer in humans a decade from now? What if viruses learn from the supposedly virus-proof plants and mutate into new diseases? What if modifications cause new allergic reactions?

If you're a North American kid, you've likely eaten a genetically modified plant today. Was there any corn in your breakfast cereal? Did that muffin at recess contain soybean or canola oil? Almost all of the corn, soybeans, and canola grown in North America are genetically modified. Health Canada and the U.S. Food and Drug Administration maintain that the products are safe.

But in Europe, governments have decided that the public's health concerns are valid. Or, at least, that the questions haven't all been answered yet. The laws of the European Union say that every single GMO product has to be thoroughly tested and approved by food-safety scientists. So far, those scientists have said okay to some animal feed. Human food has gotten a big "no, thanks." And only one genetically modified crop—a kind of corn—can be planted there.

GMOs are so new and so controversial that different laws are constantly being considered, and countries are choosing a wide range of regulations. It seems as if only time will tell who's right.

SEED WARS

ORDER IN THE COURT! On one side of the case is Farmer Joe. He's planted canola, wheat, and corn on his farm for decades, and he's committed to raising only the purest, most natural crops. On the other side of the case is Biotech Giant. It sold its genetically modified seeds to the farmers east and west of Farmer Joe's fields.

PROBLEM NUMBER ONE: Pollen from the genetically modified crops is blowing into Farmer Joe's fields. It's getting mixed up with his plants. Now they're not pure, organic, nonmodified crops. And unless he can somehow stop the wind from blowing, he can't prevent it from happening every single season.

PROBLEM NUMBER TWO: Biotech Giant has patented its GMO products. It *owns* that blowing pollen. And if its crops are now growing in Farmer Joe's field, it doesn't matter whether the wind blew the pollen or he planted genetically modified seeds himself. He's growing Biotech products, so he should have to pay Biotech for the rights.

Or should he?

Cases just like this one are making their way through North American courts. And just as soon as one court announces Farmer Joe is right, another court overturns the decision. In some cases, biotech companies have simply promised not to sue individual farmers, and the courts have accepted that compromise. But organic farmers say that's not good enough—it doesn't stop GMO pollen from blowing onto their organic fields.

If you were the judge, what would you decide?

BANKING ON GENETICS

DNA IS THE BASIC building block of life. Its spirals held the instructions for Gregor Mendel's pea plants, Walter Sutton's grasshoppers, and Thomas Hunt Morgan's fruit flies. But what if species are threatened, like the dragon's blood tree of Socotra? Their DNA—their secret codes of life—could disappear from the earth forever.

Like the dragon's blood tree, many plants are threatened by climate change. Others, from strangely colored tomato varieties to less productive wheat hybrids, are phased out as farmers switch to better-growing crops. And scientists worry that still other plants could be wiped out by diseases or natural disasters.

To ensure the world doesn't lose precious DNA diversity, researchers have founded various seed banks. These are like warehouses that can store seeds for hundreds of years. Some are dedicated to preserving seeds for food crops; others, for endangered plants. Still others are working to catalog and store as many seeds as possible from all over the world.

On an icebound island halfway between Norway and the North

Some believe these bins in the Svalbard Global Seed Vault hold the fields and meadows of the future.

Pole, the Svalbard Global Seed Vault stores its samples inside a mountain. There, seeds are buried deep within layers of rock, protected by permafrost. Even if an asteroid struck the earth, even if we all lost electrical power, the seeds within the seed vault would survive.

It's an international safe-deposit box for DNA.

ANIMAL CROSSING

LOOKING FOR A NEW PET? How about a nice glow-in-the-dark fish? It's a regular zebrafish with some extra light-reflecting cells, courtesy of a genetics lab. When it was offered for sale in the United States in 2003, it became the first genetically modified pet on the market.

These incandescent swimmers didn't start out as novelty items. Professors in Singapore and Taiwan developed the fish to help detect water pollution. When tiny amounts of pollutants were present in lakes or streams, the fish would glow.

Pet companies quickly saw the appeal of the unique creatures. After all, the pet market in Asia was booming. And people in North America already spent billions of dollars each year on fish food and cat collars, fancy doggie day cares and hamster jackets. If stores could offer unique hybrids, they might attract adventurous buyers.

Chicago artist Eduardo Kac once added genes from Pacific Northwest jellyfish to the DNA of a rabbit. Voilà! A luminescent bunny. Animal-rights activists went wild, claiming that Eduardo was playing with the basis of life, pretending to be God. But Eduardo wasn't commenting about whether the genetic modification of animals was good or bad. And scientists had already been experimenting with these technologies for some time. Eduardo simply drew an imaginary frame around the issue and presented it as art, to draw the public's attention to it. As an artist who had previously hooked himself intravenously to a robot (to symbolize the relation- ships between humans and technology) and implanted a tracking chip in his leg (to raise questions about privacy and secu- rity), Eduardo was used to stirring up controversy.

His work raised interesting questions, the same questions that many scientists, academics, animal- rights activists, ethicists, and even potential pet buyers are asking: Just how far can scientists go with crossed species and mixed-up DNA? Is it ethical to juggle with another creature's genes? Or with our own?

Genetically modified pets: a fishy business?

Some animal-rights activists argue that pets should never be genetically altered. They say that geneti- cally modifying animals in the lab is treating animals like products.

But not everyone agrees. Pet shoppers in Asia and the United States have now bought hundreds of millions of glowing fish. Apparently, they have no concerns about genetically modified pets—at least not the fishy variety.

DOUBLE TROUBLE

DO YOU KNOW ANY IDENTICAL TWINS? Can you tell them apart?

Every once in a while, after a father's sperm has fertilized a mother's egg, the resulting cell divides in two. These matching cells grow into matching fetuses and—once in every thousand births around the world—identical twins emerge.

Until fairly recently, it was believed that identical twins had identical DNA—after all, identical twins start as one fertilized egg, with one set of DNA coding. But it turns out that's not quite true. As the twins develop, long before birth, some rare DNA mutations can occur—not many, but because cells are reproducing trillions of times, a very few small differences can happen. And the environment can play a role too, before and after the twins are born, causing small but significant changes when it comes to which of their genes are working and which are inactive.

How do we know for sure that identical twins are not completely identical? They have different fingerprints!

Twins fascinate geneticists. Studying human beings is a tricky business. Usually, it's difficult to tell which traits come from DNA and which come from environment. Is it nature or nurture? For example, your

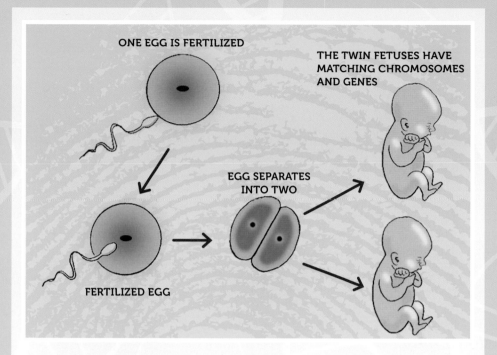

ONE EGG IS FERTILIZED

THE TWIN FETUSES HAVE MATCHING CHROMOSOMES AND GENES

EGG SEPARATES INTO TWO

FERTILIZED EGG

next-door neighbor might have a hot temper. Is that because he was born that way? Or did he have a rough childhood and develop a temper to help him cope?

Experiments with twins help scientists answer these questions. If your angry next-door neighbor has a twin brother, and that brother is calm, soft-spoken, and patient, then you can conclude that anger is not genetic. Something must have happened to your neighbor to change his personality—not his DNA.

One of the first doctors to use a "twin study" was a German skin-disease expert named Hermann Werner Siemens. In 1924, Hermann counted the number of moles on twins. He found that mole counts in identical twins were twice as similar as mole counts in fraternal twins (who share only half their DNA). He proved that moles were at least partly genetic.

No one cared too much about Hermann's moles. But researchers all over the world saw the value in his twin study. Since Hermann's time, scientists have used twins to study stress hormones, teenage smoking, lung capacity, ear deformities, eyesight, and everything in between.

By comparing twins who grew up together with twins who were adopted and grew up in different families, scientists can even study which personality traits people are born with, and which ones come from our home lives. For example, Dutch twin studies show that a love for adventure sports, like skydiving, say, is caused half by genetics and half by upbringing. Religious beliefs aren't genetic at all—those come almost entirely from family. But people who smoke are influenced by a combination of genetics, family situations, and wider environments.

Twins have been used in thousands of studies around the world. In fact, the only thing more useful than twins in scientific research is triplets. Or quadruplets. Or—wait!—what about thousands and thousands of clones?

GENETICS ROCK STAR

DOLLY THE SHEEP

CLONES ARE EXACT COPIES. Like twins, they begin as matching cells and grow into matching organisms. And that's useful for scientists because they know that all clones have exactly the same DNA. If one organism turns out differently, the reason can't be genetic.

The idea of cloning drew international attention in 1996 with the birth of Dolly the Sheep.

HOW TO CLONE A SHEEP:

- Take a normal egg cell from a sheep and scoop out its nucleus.

- Take a cell from another sheep (in Dolly's case, this egg was from a sheep's udder) and inject it into the egg cell, so that the new, combined cell has this sheep's DNA.

- Give the newly combined cell a tiny electric shock, to start it copying and dividing.

- Implant that cell into the womb of a female sheep, and watch the pregnancy progress.

This is what Ian Wilmut and his fellow Edinburgh scientists did. Dolly the Sheep was born healthy and identical to the donor of the implanted nucleus.

It had taken Ian and his crew 276 tries, but they had successfully copied their first mammal. They'd created an animal that had DNA completely identical to the DNA of the donor. With this technology, laboratories went on to produce identical copies of mice, cows, monkeys, and pigs.

An embryo is a group of cells in the very earliest stages of development. You were an embryo inside your mother's womb for the first eight weeks of her pregnancy. After that, you became a fetus.

COPIES AND CLONES

NO ONE NEEDS TO COUNT the moles or test the effects of smoking on animals. So why would anyone want identical sheep? Well, it's not about the wool. Scientists can test medicines on cloned animals and know that varying DNA doesn't affect their experiments. They can learn about animal behavior, and whether it comes from nature or nurture. But researchers in favor of cloning research say the possibilities go even further. Here are just a few of the things they hope to one day do:

- Clone human organs, so people don't have to wait on transplant lists.
- Clone cells that don't naturally regenerate, such as nerve cells, to help people recover from spinal cord injuries.
- Make healthy heart cells, then inject them into damaged hearts.
- Copy the cells of parents, so couples who can't have children naturally can have their own (genetically identical) kids.

Could genetically modified humans adapt better to space travel? Some researchers suggest that if we alter our bones for lower gravity, change our sleep rhythms to suit longer days, and strengthen our skin to resist radiation, we could survive the long journey and even adapt to life on planet Mars.

Some of these things are already underway. In 2013, scientists in Japan applied for permission to begin growing human organs inside pigs. They proposed combining human cells with pig embryos. When implanted in a pig's womb, the embryo would grow. And once the piglet was born (with a human organ inside), the organ could be removed, then transplanted into a person in need. The scientists had already successfully tried the procedure using rats and mice.

Opponents of cloning say the technology is going too far, too quickly. They say that even by cloning research animals, scientists are creating living creatures just to experiment on them and then destroy them. They also wonder what will happen if scientists start cloning human cells. Would cloned babies be used in laboratories?

Fortunately, there's no need to worry about that issue just yet—the cloning of humans has been banned by governments around the world. Even cloning human organs, as the Japanese research team proposed, hasn't yet gained support.

ON THE BRINK

IN BORNEO, palm oil is big business. To produce enough oil to feed the world's processed-food industries, loggers have hacked away the rainforest and created palm plantations.

This is great for potato chip addicts, but not such a good plan for Sumatran rhinos. They've lost their habitat. The few dozen that remain are mercilessly hunted for their horns, which are sold as medicine on the black market.

Frantic to save the animals, conservationists are trying to round up survivors, hoping they can be bred in captivity. At the Cincinnati Zoo, a rare pair has successfully produced three calves. And back in Borneo, scientists are trying to help other females conceive.

They may not be successful. There are so few animals left, and so many are injured, that it might prove impossible to save the species this way. And the rhino calves that are produced by this small parent group may be too genetically similar to build a stable population. Plus, the rhino's rainforest homes aren't growing back any time soon. Even if scientists manage to create rhino families, will they ever again roam free?

Scientists don't have all the answers, but they do have a wild backup plan. At a lab in Borneo, tissue samples from several rhinos have been carefully frozen. It's just barely possible that if geneticists learn more about cloning over the coming decades, they might be able to defrost the samples, clone the DNA, and—most difficult of all—grow new baby rhinos to term.

It's a long shot.

Restarting a species with a small selection of animals doesn't provide that important genetic diversity. And although researchers managed to clone Dolly the Sheep, experiments on endangered animals have been less successful. In 2000, a lab in Massachusetts gathered samples from a male gaur, or Indian bison, native to Southeast Asia. They attempted to clone the animal. They implanted 692 nucleuses into healthy egg cells. Eighty-one of those began to divide and

develop. Forty-two managed to grow into embryos and were implanted in female cows. Eight cows became pregnant. Only one delivered a healthy baby gaur.

Little Noah, the gaur, was the first successfully cloned endangered animal. Unfortunately, he died from an infection two days after his birth.

While results are slowly improving, cloning at-risk species is still a compli- cated and expensive process. Many conservationists say it would be better to use the money and energy to preserve habitat. Or to save creatures with better chances of survival in the wild.

BACK TO THE FUTURE

WOOLLY MAMMOTHS once again roaming the Arctic. Dodoes populat- ing islands in the Indian Ocean. Saber-toothed tigers gnashing their fangs at zoo visitors.

In 2008, researchers used the remains of several long-dead woolly mammoths to sequence the creature's genome. For the first time, they had a complete DNA picture of an extinct animal. This got the world wondering. Could a live mammoth be the next step?

Not any time soon, apparently. There are a few problems to consider. First, DNA degrades after death, so the samples used by scientists weren't perfect. If they tried to recreate a mammoth from the sequence they have now, the animal would have hundreds of thousands of mutations.

It would never develop properly. And even if scientists could create a strong, pure copy, there would be several other challenges:

- How many chromosomes does a mammoth have? The same as an elephant? Researchers have no idea.

- The mammoth DNA would have to be added to other cells—probably from frogs (which have cells that are extra-good at adapting to foreign DNA) or elephants (the best mammoth look-alikes). The cells would need to divide and grow. No one knows if that would work.

- Some sort of live animal would need to carry the pregnancy. Could an elephant mom birth a baby mammoth?

Obviously, there are lots of questions to be answered before woolly mammoths walk the earth again. But will it one day be possible? It might be too strange, too complicated, and too expensive. Then again, that's exactly what people said about walking on the moon.

NEVER SEEN CREATURES WITH SKIS BEFORE. MUST BE SOME OF THOSE NEW GMOS.

IF ONLY ONE PERSON ROBBED THE JEWELRY STORE, BUT THE TWINS HAVE NEARLY IDENTICAL DNA, HOW WILL THE DETECTIVE SOLVE THE CRIME?

PIA NUTT
SUPERMODEL,
REGULAR CUSTOMER

HAZEL NUTT
SUPERMODEL,
REGULAR CUSTOMER

HINT: It will be *nearly* impossible. Turn to page 107 to find out more.

WHODUNIT? 6

GENETICISTS HAVE BEEN doing wild and wonderful things with their genome know-how. Here are just a few discoveries:

- Scientists have traced all of humanity back to one region of Africa.
- They've tested Egyptian mummies to figure out the family trees of ancient pharaohs.
- They've scraped skeleton teeth for DNA in the bacteria that caused the plague.

But while all of this is interesting to read about, it doesn't really affect our daily lives—or does it?

We don't necessarily think about our DNA when we visit the doctor's office, drive by the police station, or meet a long-lost cousin. But genetics are at work in all three places. And for some people, genetic research has been life-changing and even life-saving. Geneticists are helping cure disease, solve crimes, and reunite families. All of these things are probably happening right in your own town or city, right now.

BURSTING THE BUBBLE

IN 2001, young Rhys Evans was rushed to the hospital near his home in South Wales. He had pneumonia. Doctors tried an oxygen tent, but he still wasn't getting enough air. In desperation, they turned to a ventilator to force oxygen into his lungs.

Rhys had something known as "boy in the bubble" disease. Blood tests had revealed a defective gene. Because of that gene, he couldn't make his own white blood cells, so his body couldn't fend off germs. But when Rhys was transferred to a sterile room at Great Ormond Street Hospital in London, doctors there offered a tiny hope.

Thanks to their new understanding of how genes worked, scientists had found a way to inject a healthy human gene into a mouse retrovirus. A retrovirus is a miniature parasite. It invades healthy cells and tricks them into copying virus code. If the retrovirus were altered to carry a healthy human gene, then when it invaded cells, it could make those cells copy the new gene.

The treatment had worked in French trials two years before. Rhys would be the English hospital's first attempt of it. Did his parents want to try?

Desperate, they agreed. The doctors embarked on their groundbreaking procedure:

- They extracted cells from Rhys's blood marrow.
- They genetically engineered the mouse retrovirus to carry the human gamma-c gene.
- They mixed the retrovirus cells with Rhys's blood marrow cells.
- They injected the cocktail back into Rhys's system.

Then they waited. Slowly, the little boy's lungs began to clear. His body started producing white blood cells. A few months later, the toddler could play with other kids and run in the park—things he'd never done before.

Rhys became one of the first patients to be saved by genetic engineering. And as scientists increased their understanding of how genes worked—and even how to fix them—more and more people would benefit.

WARNING SIGNS

ARE YOU A MUTANT? Well, you may not have razor claws or super-speed like the X-Men mutants, but you do have mutations within you. Since every person has a unique genetic code of more than 3 billion units, a few of those units are bound to be mixed up.

Usually, these mix-ups are harmless. The healthy parts of your DNA code balance out any problems. But what if you have a family history of a genetic disease, a mutation that's been passed down through generations?

Women with a family history of breast cancer can now undergo a genetic test to tell them whether they have a mutation in their BRCA1 gene. That gene is a sort of caretaker. It's responsible for making a protein to repair damaged DNA. Without a properly working BRCA1 gene, a woman's body doesn't have the proper repair services, and tumor cells can begin to multiply. She has a 65 percent chance of developing breast cancer—often while she's still young.

Women with a family history of breast cancer often choose to have genetic testing because there are things that can be done to make cancer

Your genes have probably been tested. In hospitals, North American newborns are automatically assessed for at least two genetic disorders—one called PKU (short for phenylketonuria), which can cause brain damage, and one that causes a thyroid problem. If those disorders are caught early, they're easily treatable.

less likely. In some cases, they can have preventative radiation treatments. Other women choose surgery.

But what if you have a family history of something with less obvious treatments? For example, some people have tests to tell them whether they're at risk of early-onset dementia. A defective gene might mean they have a greater chance of losing their memory while they're still in their fifties or sixties. But there's not much they can do to change their fate, even if they know. So, is it better to know?

What would you decide?

SWITCHED ON

IN RECENT DECADES, scientists have discovered something startling about our genes. Whether or not we have a particular gene isn't always the only thing that matters. Sometimes what matters is whether or not our gene is working. That's one of the reasons identical twins can end up with slight differences.

The DNA in our cells teams up with proteins and chemical tags. Some of these proteins and chemicals are like light switches. They control genes, turning them on or off. The on/off changes don't affect the structure of DNA. Each cell still has the same instructions. But the switches *do* determine which parts of the instructions are used.

The study of our microscopic light switches is called "epigenetics." And epigenetics explains all sorts of strange things about our bodies. For instance:

- Our cells have the same DNA, but blood cells are round and fat, while nerve cells are long and thin. How do they grow differently?

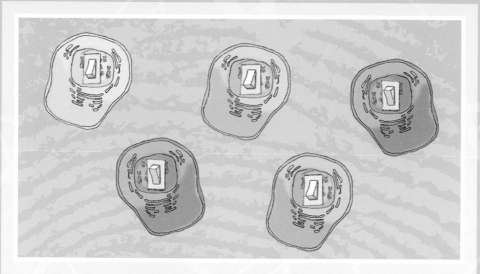

- Two identical twins live in the same home for their entire lives. But only one develops diabetes. Why?

- When mother mice are fed vitamins, the fur color of their babies changes.

  Vitamins don't change DNA, so what's happening?
  Epigenetics.
  In each of these cases, "light switches" are telling cells which genes to use and which genes to ignore.

Scientists don't always understand why our genes are turned on or off. There's much more research to be done. But many think it has to do with our habits and our environments. Maybe the diabetic twin ate a lot of candy as a child, and that made her gene instructions work differently. Or maybe she took strong medicines, lived for a year in a different country, or worked in a stressful job. Any of these things could affect a person's on/off switches.

As they understand epigenetics better, researchers may be able to discover chemicals that can switch genes back on, or turn them off. Even now, some labs are experimenting with medicines custom-designed for people's specific epigenetic changes.

GENERATION GAPS

HERE'S ONE OF THE STRANGEST things about epigenetics: the on/off gene changes might transfer from parent to child.

This is easy to prove in plants. If a wild radish plant is attacked by caterpillars, it grows prickly bits and gives off bad odors. Anything to chase those caterpillars away! The plant hasn't experienced a gene mutation. Instead, some of its on/off switches have changed.

That's when things get mysterious. The next generation of baby radishes also has prickly bits and bad smells, even if those plants are never touched by caterpillars. The parent plants have somehow passed their epigenetic changes to the baby plants.

The same sort of thing may happen in humans. For example, researchers studied harvest records from a town in northern Sweden. When young boys in the late 1800s and early 1900s had plenty of food,

their modern-day sons and grandsons had higher rates of heart disease and diabetes. When long-ago boys experienced bad harvest years and ate a little less food, their descendants were healthier.

Weird but true. The researchers suggest that when the boys overate, they changed their epigenetics. Their bodies got used to extra food. Those epigenetics were passed to sons and to grandsons, causing generations of overeating boys. Extra food led to extra weight, and eventually to higher rates of heart disease and diabetes.

It's difficult to prove these sorts of epigenetic changes in humans because we have complicated genomes and long lifespans. Obviously, it's easier to track wild radishes than human families. But many scientists are sure that epigenetics are affecting people's daily lives, and might even affect future generations.

GENETICS ROCK STAR

SUPER SLEUTH

HOW ELSE MIGHT GENES AFFECT our days? Well, that depends on whether you're planning to commit a crime this week. If you are, you might want to review the work of a British scientist named Alec Jeffreys.

In 1984, Alec was examining X-ray films of DNA. He'd been doing the same thing for years, and he'd seen patterns from baboons, lemurs, seals, cows, mice, rats, frogs, people, and plants. On this particular morning, he was looking at DNA films of a human family, searching for two things: markers called "minisatellites" that could mark a core area for comparison, and the sequence of DNA around those minisatellites.

Suddenly, Alec realized that the strands he was examining had distinct similarities and differences—and that the similarities could be used to link family members, while the differences could work as "fingerprints" to identify individuals.

He'd discovered what would soon become known as DNA fingerprinting.

After a British newspaper reported on the new technique, Alec received a call from a lawyer in London. Immigration authorities were about to deport a boy. While his family was allowed to stay in England, the boy was about to be sent back to Ghana. Apparently, his blood tests had shown that he was related *somehow* to the rest of the family but hadn't shown that he was necessarily the son. He could have been a cousin or a nephew.

Could Alec help?

With his new DNA fingerprinting technique, Alec was able to prove that mother and son were indeed members of the same immediate family. The deportation case was dropped, the boy was allowed to remain in England, and DNA fingerprinting had solved its first legal case.

In 2014, the city of Naples, Italy, announced it would be using DNA to identify dog poop left on the sidewalks. All dogs must be registered, and then a blood sample is taken, providing a DNA fingerprint. When poop is found on the sidewalk, it's sent to the lab for analysis. And if there's a DNA match between the poop and your pooch, you'll have a fine to pay!

GUILTY UNTIL PROVEN INNOCENT

IN 1970, seventeen-year-old David Milgaard was convicted of murdering a young nursing assistant, Gail Miller, in Saskatchewan. Although he insisted he was innocent, David was sentenced to life in prison. His appeal was denied. And after that, his life started to seem like a crime novel:

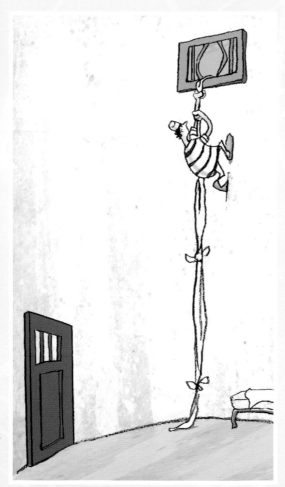

1973: He escaped from prison, only to be captured and returned.

1980: He escaped again. This time he was shot in the back, then returned.

1991: The justice minister said she wouldn't reopen his case.

1992: David was released from jail, but not declared innocent. Thanks to campaigning by his mother and intervention by the prime minister, the Supreme Court of Canada agreed to a review.

1997: DNA evidence proved David was innocent.

In the past decade, DNA has proven the innocence of more than fifteen death-row inmates in the United States—people who were about to die for their crimes. Activists worry that in cases where DNA evidence is not used, prisoners might be executed unfairly. They argue that all states should have clear laws to ensure DNA evidence is taken, used, and properly stored.

David Milgaard spent some twenty-two years behind bars. The province of Saskatchewan gave him $10 million for his trouble.

And the DNA evidence that exonerated him? It pointed to another suspect, a man who'd committed similar crimes in the past. Once again, Alec Jeffrey's DNA fingerprinting had solved a crime. Since 1984, his techniques have been used in millions of crime investigations around the world.

BODIES OF EVIDENCE

AFTER A TSUNAMI HIT Southeast Asia on December 26, 2004, more than 280,000 people died. In Phuket, Thailand, many of the dead were tourists—visitors from Asia, Europe, and North America who'd flocked to the island beaches to enjoy a winter holiday in the sun.

The tragedy left their families in far-flung corners of the world wondering what exactly had happened. They couldn't fly to Phuket—the region was in shambles. They were left scanning the TV news for clues. Were their relatives confirmed dead? Were they lost at sea, or left on the beaches? What if they were alive and injured?

Along with medical and rescue professionals, China sent a four-person team of DNA experts to help. These experts could test up to

The South Asian tsunami of 2004 strikes a beach in Thailand.

4,500 bodies a day and create a database showing the DNA of the dead. In other parts of the world, if family members chose to have their own DNA analyzed, they could then compare it to the online database. They'd discover, once and for all, if their relatives were among the tsunami's many victims.

CATALOG CONCERNS

AROUND THE WORLD, governments and police forces are keeping bigger and bigger databases of DNA. It's so useful! They can track criminals that way. Let's say someone named Sam robs a store when he's twenty years old. He's caught and convicted, and his DNA is filed. Ten years later, the police investigate a murder and find DNA evidence at the scene. When it matches Sam's DNA in the database, they know that Sam is a likely suspect.

Now imagine a slightly more complicated situation. Maybe the police find DNA at a crime scene and it doesn't match any known criminals. But they find a partial match to Sam's DNA. If the chromosomes are XX, they know that they're looking for one of Sam's female relatives; if they find XY, it's a male relative of Sam's.

In the DNA mystery within this book, a detective has rounded up suspects and asked each person to give a DNA sample. Only one person is guilty, but now all of them might have DNA stored in a database.

Is this a good thing? It might make it easier for the police to solve future crimes. But what if a government decides to use its DNA database for other things? It could give away the information to scientists, or let insurance companies peek at which people are likely to get cancer—all without permission.

In some countries, activists are working to protect people's DNA privacy. But it's such a new field, there are plenty of loopholes. So, if you were a suspect in this jewelry store robbery, should you give the police your DNA? In some countries, you'd be legally required to. In other countries, you'd have the right to choose. And in still others, a judge might decide based on the circumstances.

If you were a suspect, what would you decide?

I'VE FOUND A DNA TEST SO SENSITIVE IT CAN FIND THE TINIEST DIFFERENCES IN DNA SEQUENCING. IT CAN EVEN READ EPIGENETIC CHANGES. THIS IS THE ONLY TEST THAT CAN SPOT THE DIFFERENCE BETWEEN IDENTICAL TWINS.

YOU'RE TALKING ABOUT THAT NEWFANGLED, EXTRA-DETAILED DNA TEST. THOSE ARE EXPENSIVE.

NOT AS EXPENSIVE AS THE STOLEN JEWELS. AND WE'VE SOLVED THE CASE: THE DNA INSIDE THE GLOVE IS THAT OF PIA NUTT. SHE'LL HAVE A LOT OF EXPLAINING TO DO IN COURT.

APPARENTLY, PIA HAS BEEN OVER-SPENDING FOR YEARS AND SHE'S BROKE. BUT SHE COULDN'T STAND TO BE SEEN IN FEWER JEWELS THAN HER SISTER. SO SHE DECIDED TO STEAL SOME EXTRA. THIS CASE IS CLOSED!

CONCLUSION

THE NEXT CASE

CRIME FIGHTER OF THE YEAR! Using DNA know-how, the detective narrowed the list of jewelry store suspects. She found DNA evidence at the crime scene. She used genetic information to rule out a color-blind suspect, and cleared another based on DNA evidence stored by law enforcement. Once the lab provided all the evidence, she eliminated suspects who were male, then those of non-Scandinavian descent. And finally, she used the latest in DNA fingerprinting technology to find the thief: supermodel Pia Nutt.

DNA fingerprinting has made huge changes to how the police investigate crimes. But, as you now know, genetics research affects our lives in countless other ways. Scientists are just beginning to explore the possibilities. In coming years, they'll be researching ways to lengthen the human lifespan, address challenges in food production and world hunger, and help preserve endangered species.

While we can all agree that DNA fingerprinting is helpful, how many of its potential applications are positive? How many come with risks? And who's deciding which are which?

The first eliminated suspect is Dr. Hacker, at the end of Chapter 2.

Terry Bill disappears after Chapter 3.

At the end of chapter 4, three people are eliminated because they're male: Rusty Hammer, Stan Still, and Dwayne Pipe. Also, we lose anyone who doesn't appear Scandinavian: Dee Zaster, Daisy Picker, and Ida Gottaway.

At the end of Chapter 5, we know it's one of the twins.

At the end of Chapter 6, we identify the thief as Pia Nutt.

103

Have a look at these three ethical dilemmas and try to decide . . . where would you draw the line?

GENETIC DISEASE

Scientists can now discover who might be at risk of developing a disease with a genetic basis. What if . . .

- Women who are at a greater risk of breast cancer choose early treatment—whether they will ultimately develop cancer or not?

- Teens find out they're at risk of Huntington's disease, a deadly mental disorder with no cure?

- Companies and labs that perform the tests store databases with everyone's DNA results?

- Insurance companies access genetic records and refuse life insurance to people at risk of rare conditions?

TECHNO BABIES

Doctors can now discover genetic information about babies while they are still in the womb. What if . . .

- Parents choose to abort children with genetic disorders such as Down syndrome?

- Parents choose to keep boy babies and abort girls, or vice versa?

- Parents demand that researchers create genetic modifications to make their babies taller, stronger, and smarter?

DNA FINGERPRINTING

Police now collect and store DNA evidence from crimes that cause serious harm to people—crimes such as murder. What if . . .

- Police create larger databanks, storing the DNA of all major criminals?
- Even people suspected of minor crimes have their DNA cataloged?
- Countries create massive DNA databases of all citizens?
- Hackers steal the information and use other people's DNA to steal their identities, or to plant false evidence at crime scenes?

Some of these situations are already happening. Others seem a little far-fetched, but with genetic research speeding ahead, they could soon become real dilemmas. And in DNA research, some of the strangest stories have roots in truth.

TWIN TRUTHS

SO, INVESTIGATORS HAVE solved the crime! In this story, the jewelry store was robbed by one of the identical twins: Pia Nutt.

Could this sort of mystery occur in real life? Apparently, yes.

On January 25, 2009, someone stole millions of dollars' worth of jewelry from a high-end department store in Berlin. It was a heist that seemed straight out of a Hollywood movie. The thieves climbed through a second-floor window, dropped a rope ladder to the floor, then nimbly ducked the motion detectors and alarm sensors as they cracked open jewelry display cases.

They escaped the building, and no one realized the store had been robbed until early the next morning. When the police were called, they

found two clues at the scene: a rope ladder and a single glove. From the glove, they extracted a DNA sample, and the sample led them straight to . . . twins.

They arrested two twenty-seven-year-olds, Abbas and Hassan O. (In Germany, crime suspects are identified in the media only by their last initial.) The police were stumped. Abbas said it must have been Hassan who robbed the store. Hassan said it was Abbas. And the DNA samples couldn't show the difference.

A newfangled research technique could probably have given the police their answer. Researchers had recently come up with a highly sensitive (and highly expensive) way to distinguish between the DNA of twins. But the research was so new, it wasn't allowed by the rules of German courts.

No charges could be laid. It was the perfect crime.

FURTHER READING

Eamer, Claire. *Spiked Scorpions & Walking Whales*. Toronto: Annick Press, 2009.

———. *Super Crocs & Monster Wings*. Toronto: Annick Press, 2008.

Loxton, Daniel. *Evolution*. Toronto: Kids Can Press, 2010.

Marx, Christy. *Watson and Crick and DNA*. New York: Rosen Publishing Group, 2005.

Morrison, Yvonne. *The DNA Gave It Away!* New York: Scholastic, 2008.

Owen, David. *Hidden Evidence*. Buffalo, NY: Firefly Books, 2009.

Schultz, Mark. *The Stuff of Life*. New York: Hill and Wang, 2009.

Seiple, Samantha, and Todd Seiple. *Mutants, Clones, and Killer Corn*. Minneapolis, MN: Lerner Publishing Group, 2005.

Simpson, Kathleen. *Genetics: From DNA to Designer Dogs*. Washington, DC: National Geographic Children's Books, 2008.

SELECTED SOURCES

Boomsma, Dorrett, A. Busjahn, and L. Peltonen. "Classical twin studies and beyond." *Nature Reviews Genetics*, November 2002, 872–82.

Boyhan, Diane, and Henry Daniell. "Low-cost production of proinsulin in tobacco and lettuce chloroplasts for injectable or oral delivery of functional insulin and C-peptide." *Plant Biotechnology Journal*, June 2011, 585–98.

Chuan, Qin. "Beijing tests DNA from Thailand." *China Daily*, January 6, 2005, 1.

Cobb, Matthew. "Heredity before genetics: A history." *Nature Reviews Genetics*, December 2006, 953–58.

Complete Dictionary of Scientific Biography. Detroit: Charles Scribner's Sons, 2008.

Connor, Steve. "Doctors claim a first genetic 'cure' for Rhys, the boy in the bubble." *Independent*, April 4, 2002, 3.

Elkin, Lynne Osman. "Rosalind Franklin and the double helix." *Physics Today*, March 2003, 42.

Epstein, David. *The Sports Gene*. New York: Current, 2013.

Flam, Faye. "Cancer and Tasmanian devils." *Philadelphia Inquirer*, July 4, 2011, C01.

Friedberg, Errol C. "Maurice Wilkins (1916–2004)." *Molecular Cell*, December 3, 2004, 671–72.

Gill, Tony. "The atomic fish." *Humanist*, September–October 2004, 7–9.

Glynn, Jenifer. "Rosalind Franklin: 50 years on." *Notes & Records of the Royal Society*, 2008, 253–55.

Gratzer, Walter. "Obituary: Maurice Wilkins (1916–2004)." *Nature*, October 21, 2004, 922.

Haldane, John B. S. *Possible Worlds*. London: Chatto & Windus, 1927.

Hass, L. F. "Gregor Johann Mendel (1822–84)." *Journal of Neurology, Neurosurgery, and Psychiatry*, May 1998, 587.

Hawkes, Nigel. "Crick answered when immortality knocked." *London Times*, July 30, 2004, 38.

Herrera, Stephan. "Profile: Eduardo Kac." *Nature Biotechnology*, November 2005, 1331.

Hodgkinson, Kathy, E. Dicks, S. Connors, T.-L. Young, P. Parfey, and D. Pullman. "Translation of research discoveries to clinical care in arrhythmogenic right ventricular cardiomyopathy in Newfoundland and Labrador". *Genetics in Medicine*, December 2009, 859–65.

Hyde, Natalie. *DNA*. New York: Crabtree Publishing, 2010.

Iyer, V. Ramesh, and A. J. Chin. "Arrhythmogenic right ventricular cardiomyopathy/dysplasia (ARVC/D)." *American Journal of Medical Genetics*, August 2013, 185–97.

Jegalian, Karin, and Bruce T. Lahn. "Why the Y is so weird." *Scientific American*, February 2001, 56–61.

Jeffreys, Alec J. "Genetic fingerprinting." *Nature Medicine*, October 2005, 1035–39.

Kariminejad, Mohammad H., and Ardeshir Khorshidian. "Science of breeding and heredity from ancient Persia to modern Iran." *Indian Journal of Human Genetics*, January–April 2012, 34–39.

Kieran, Mark W., Leslie Gordon, and Monica Kleinman. "New approaches to progeria." *Pediatrics*, October 1, 2007, 834–41.

Kulish, Nicholas. "Fork at end of DNA road in Berlin jewelry robbery." *International New York Times*, February 21, 2009, 2.

Luzzatto, Lucio. "Sickle cell anaemia and malaria." *Mediterranean Journal of Hematology and Infectious Diseases* 4, 1 (2012), e2012065.

McCallum, Hamish. "Tasmanian devil facial tumor disease: Lessons for conservation ecology." *Trends in Ecology and Evolution*, November 2008, 631–37.

Monsanto. "Company History." Accessed March 3, 2014. http://www.monsanto.com/whoweare/Pages/monsanto-history.aspx.

Nathans, J., D. Thomas, and D.S. Hogess. "Molecular genetics of human color vision." *Lancet*, February 3, 1990, 263–64.

National Human Genome Research Institute. "All About the Human Genome Project." Accessed February 25, 2014. http://www.genome.gov/10001772.

Nicholls, Henry. "Darwin 200: Let's make a mammoth." *Nature*, November 2008, 310–14.

———. "Endangered species: Sex and the single rhinoceros." *Nature*, May 31, 2012, 566–69.

Offner, Susan. "The Y chromosome." *American Biology Teacher*, April 1, 2010, 235–40.

Pitman, Joanna. "Watson, Crick and the DNA double helix." *London Times*, April 19, 2008, 6.

Sindaco, R., M. Metallinou, D. Pupin, M. Fasola, and S. Carranza. "Forgotten in the ocean." *Zoologica Scripta*, July 2012, 346–62.

Stockman, James A. III. "Clinical facts and curios." *Current Problems in Pediatric and Adolescent Health Care*, August 2007, 287–93.

Toronto Star. "David Milgaard chronology." *Toronto Star*, November 30, 1991, A9.

White, Mel. "Where the weird things are." *National Geographic*, June 1, 2012, 122.

Williams, Sarah C. P. "Epigenetics." *Proceedings of the National Academy of Sciences*, February 26, 2013, 3209.

IMAGE CREDITS

INDEX

adenine 4, 24, 46, 48, 50
Africa 16, 63, 64, 88
Amazon 11
anemia 34–36
animals 3, 15, 27, 81–82
    Chamaeleo monachus 27
    cheetahs 16
    dingoes 15
    dogs 96
    Dolly the Sheep 80–81, 84
    gaurs 84–85
    genetically modified 69–71, 76–77
    pets 76–77
    rabbits 77
    sheep 8–9, 80–81, 82
    Sumatran rhinoceroses 83–84
    Sunda pangolins 40
    Tasmanian devils 15–16
    woolly mammoths 85–86
    See also birds, fish
Argentina 11
Aristotle 8
Asia 40, 64, 76, 78, 84, 98–99
Australia 15–16

Bakewell, Robert 8
Barrington Brown, Antony 51
Beagle 11
Berlin, Germany 106–107
Berns, Sam 37–38
Berns, Scott 38
biotechnology 70, 74–75
birds 15
    brown kiwis 39
    finches 13–14, 39
    pigeons 13–14
blood 34–36, 40, 49, 50, 89, 92
    See also anemia, hemophilia
Borneo 83–84
Boston Bruins 37
Bridges, Calvin Blackman 32
Britain 58
    See also England

brown kiwis 39

Cambridge University 44, 49
Canada 97–98
cancer 16, 73, 90–91, 104
canola 73
Celera Corporation 58, 60
cells 5, 24, 30, 50, 82, 92
    division 25, 45, 78
    egg 8, 78
    nucleus 24
    sperm 8, 78
    See also chromosomes
Chara, Zdeno 37
Chargaff, Erwin 50
Charles II, King of Spain 10
cheetahs 16
China 8, 58, 98–99
chromosomes 24, 25, 30, 33, 86
    Y chromosome 31–32, 33
Cincinnati Zoo 84
climate change 28
cloning 69, 80–85
    Dolly the Sheep 80–81, 84
    endangered species 83–85, 102
    extinct animals 85–86
    organs 82–83
Collins, Francis 61
color blindness 36–37
Columbia University 32
corn 73
Coulson, Alan 57
Crayola Crayons 36
Crick, Francis 49–52, 56
crops 7
cytosine 4, 24, 46, 48, 50

Dalai Lama 63
Daniell, Henry 71
Darwin, Charles 11–14, 15, 28, 29, 32, 39
deoxyribose 4
desert rose 27, 28
de Vries, Hugo 21

diabetes 55, 71, 93, 95
    See also insulin
dingoes 15
DNA databases 99–100, 104, 105
DNA fingerprinting 5, 23, 95–99, 102, 105
Dolly the Sheep 80–81, 84
Down syndrome 104
dragon's blood tree 27, 28, 75

Ecuador 11, 14
Egypt 88
embryos 32, 81, 83
endangered species 83–85, 102
England 8, 10, 11, 43, 47, 49, 89, 96
    See also Britain
enzymes 46
epigenetics 92–95
Europe 10, 73, 98
Evans, Rhys 89–90
evidence 3, 5, 97–98, 99–100, 102, 105, 107
exonucleolytic proofreading 46

families 5, 7, 8, 10, 95–96
farming 7
finches 13–14, 39
fingerprints 3, 5, 78
    See also DNA fingerprinting
fish
    genetically modified 76–78
    icefish 40
    Pacific Northwest jellyfish 77
    zebrafish 76
flies 33
Food and Drug Administration 73
France 9, 58
Franklin, Rosalind 43–45, 47, 49, 50, 52

Galápagos Islands 11–14, 28–19
    finches 13–14
gaurs 84–85
gender 31–33
genes 24, 25, 33, 37, 55–56, 62
    dominant 19
    epigenetics 92–95
    genetic engineering 89–90
    ownership of 58–60
    recessive 19
    See also Human Genome Project,
    genetically modified organisms
genetic disease 37–38, 89–91, 104

genetic engineering 89–90, 104
genetic testing 90–91, 95–96
genetically modified organisms (GMOs)
    69–70, 72–73, 76–78
Germany 10, 58, 106–107
Ghana 96
Gordon, Leslie 38
Great Ormond Street Hospital 89
guanine 4, 24, 46, 48, 50

Habsburg jaw 10
Haldane, J. B. S. 34–36
Health Canada 73
heart disease 65–66, 95
hemophilia 10
HERITAGE project 62
Hippocrates 8
Human Genome Project 54–55, 57–58, 60,
    61, 62, 63, 66
Huntington's disease 104

icefish 40
Iceland 66–67
insulin 56, 71
Italy 96

Japan 58, 83
Jeffreys, Alec 95–96, 98

Kac, Eduardo 77
Khan, Genghis 64

law of independent assortment 19
law of segregation 19
Levene, Phoebus 21
Levine, Adam 63
livestock 7, 8
London, England 43, 47, 49, 89, 96

malaria 35–36
Mars 83
Maupertuis, Pierre Louis 9
Mediterranean 34
Mendel, Gregor 18–20, 29, 32, 39, 69, 70, 75
microscopes 8, 25, 47
Miescher, Friedrich 21
migration 63
Milgaard, David 97–98
Miller, Gail 97
mitosis. *See* cells: division

Monsanto 70
Morgan, Thomas Hunt 32–33, 39, 55, 75
Moser, Emerson 36–37
Muller, Hermann Joseph 32
mutations 21, 26–29, 34, 35, 36–38, 40,
    63–64, 65–66, 78, 89–91
    in flies 33, 55–56

National Center for Human Genome
    Research 57–58, 61
natural selection 14
New Zealand 39
Newfoundland 65–66
Nobel Prize 33, 50, 52, 56–57
North America 73
North Pole 75
Norway 75
nuclein 21
nucleotides 4, 24
nucleus 24, 25

On the Origin of the Species 14

Pacific Northwest jellyfish 77
palindromes 47–48
patents 59–60
Pauling, Linus 50
pets 76–78
phosphate 4, 24
pigeons 13–14
plants 7, 11, 26, 17–20, 34
    canola 73
    corn 73
    desert rose 27, 28
    dragon's blood tree 27, 75
    genetically modified 70–71
    peas 17–20, 75
    primroses 21
    soybeans 73
    tomatoes 75
    wheat 75
    wild radishes 94
progeria 37–38
Progeria Research Foundation 38

rabbits 77
religion 48
Rowling, J. K. 63
Russia 10
Sanger, Frederick 56–57

Scandinavia 64
seed banks 75–76
seeds 8
    genetically modified 74–75
    seed banks 75–76
sheep 8–9, 82
    Dolly the Sheep 80–81
Siemens, Hermann Werner 79
Singapore 76
Socotra 26–28, 34, 75
South America 11, 64
soybeans 73
space travel 83
Spain 10
Spencer, Herbert 14
Sturtevant, Alfred Henry 32, 55–56, 57
Sumatran rhinoceroses 83–84
Sunda pangolins 40
survival of the fittest 14, 29
Sutton, Walter 30, 32, 39, 75
Svalbard Global Seed Vault 75–76
Sweden 94–95

Taiwan 76
Tasmanian devils 15–16
Thailand 98–99
thymine 4, 24, 46, 48, 50
twins 5, 78–80, 93, 107

United States 76

Victoria, Queen 10
viruses 44, 73

Watson, James 47, 49–52, 56
Wilkins, Maurice 47, 49, 52
Wilmut, Ian 81
Wilson, E. B. 30
woolly mammoths 85–86
World War I 34

X-ray crystallography 43–44, 47, 49

Yemen 26

ABOUT THE AUTHOR AND ILLUSTRATOR

TANYA LLOYD KYI comes from a long genetic line of storytellers, though most of those relatives told their tales at family barbecues. Perhaps a DNA mutation prompted Tanya to put *her* stories on paper. She's now written more than 15 books for middle-grade and young-adult readers, on topics ranging from poison to underwear. Tanya lives in Vancouver, British Columbia, with her husband and their two children.

In addition to illustrating more than a dozen children's books, LIL CRUMP has created artwork for magazines, T-shirts, greeting cards, posters, and games, as well as paintings for art gallery shows. If there is an empty surface, Lil will draw or paint on it. Lil lives with her husband, daughter, and yellow dog, creating fun stuff from her studio overlooking St. Margarets Bay in Nova Scotia.

The Adventures of Medical Man: Kids' Illnesses and Injuries Explained

By Dr. Michael Evans and David Wichman
Illustrated by Gareth Williams

"This book does a fantastic job of explaining common medical issues in an accessible way. While the stories are inventive and entertaining, the medical facts are at the forefront, and readers will come away thinking about these conditions in a whole new way."— *School Library Journal*

Paperback $12.95
Hardcover $21.95

Seeing Red: The True Story of Blood

By Tanya Lloyd Kyi • Illustrated by Steve Rolston

* YALSA Quick Picks List

"In this gory, compelling overview of the nature of blood, fascinated readers will find a great deal of information and lots of laughs to help the medicine go down."—*Resource Links*

Paperback $14.95
Hardcover $22.95

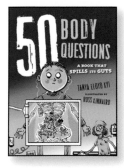

50 Body Questions: A Book That Spills Its Guts

By Tanya Lloyd Kyi • Illustrated by Ross Kinnaird

* Best Books for Kids & Teens 2014, Canadian Children's Book Centre
* Silver Birch Award nomination, Ontario Library Association

"A tour (de force) through the human body that's eminently understandable and entertaining and even often quite funny."
— *Kirkus, starred review*

Paperback $14.95
Hardcover $22.95

Patient Zero: Solving the Mysteries of Deadly Epidemics

By Marilee Peters

"The book reads like a thriller, with gripping accounts of how these diseases affected people."— *School Library Journal*

"The mysterious nature of unexplained epidemics is perfectly captured."— *Kirkus Reviews*

Paperback $14.95
Hardcover $24.95